JavaScript: The Fundamentals

Cristian Salcescu

JavaScript
The Fundamentals

JavaScript: The Fundamentals

Cristian Salcescu

ISBN-13: 979-8466335996

History:

September 2021 First Edition

January 2022 Revision

Contents

Preface

JavaScript is the language of the web and one of the most used programming languages.

It puts together some powerful features like closures, functions as values, objects as dynamic collections of properties, experimental characteristics, the prototype system, and some dangerous features such as the type coercion system.

This book looks at the fundamental concepts in the JavaScript language. It covers the basic units like numbers, strings, booleans, objects, functions, arrays, sets, maps, dates and regular expressions. It compares objects with maps, arrow functions with function declarations, strings with arrays of characters.

The book ends with the language's core features, making it unique in a sense.

Enjoy the learning journey!

Source Code

The source code is available at
https://github.com/cristi-salcescu/javascript-the-fundamentals.

Feedback

I will be glad to hear your feedback. For comments, questions, or suggestions regarding this book send me an email to cristisalcescu@gmail.com. Thanks in advance for considering to write a review of the book.

Chapter 01: Values and Variables

Variables, values, and types are the core concepts of a language. The first chapter makes a quick introduction of these notions making it easier to understand the detailed information in the next chapters.

Primitives

Primitive values represent data like numbers or texts. Below are few examples.

```
1
"Hi!"
true
```

Every value has a type. The primitive types are number, bigint, string, boolean, symbol, undefined, and null.

The value 1 is a number primitive created using the number literal.

The "Hi!" value is a string. Strings are surrounded by single-quotes, double-quotes, or the backtick character.

The boolean type has two values `true` and `false`.

Undefined is a type with a single value, `undefined`. Similarly, null is a type with a single value `null`.

We can detect the type of a value using the `typeof` operator.

```
typeof 1        //"number"
typeof "Hello"  //"string"
typeof true     //"boolean"
```

```
typeof undefined  //"undefined"
```

The double slash // symbol marks a comment. The text after it till the end of the line is a comment. A text between /* and */ is also treated as a comment and can span several lines.

```
/*
The Main
JavaScript
Types
*/
```

Objects

An object is a dynamic collection of properties. A property has a name and a value.

Here is a simple object storing a single property with the name number and the value 1.

```
const obj = {
  number : 1
}
```

The type of an object is as expected 'object'.

```
typeof obj //"object"
```

Arrays are collections of values and are also considered objects.

Below is an array of numbers.

```
[1, 2, 3]
```

We can basically split the types into two, primitives and objects. Any value that is not primitive is an object.

Functions

A function is a piece of code that is defined once, can be named and parameterized, and then is invoked when needed.

Functions are reusable blocks of code.

Here is an example of defining a piece of logic multiplying two numbers and having the name multiply.

```
function multiply(a, b) {
  return a * b;
}
```

We can then call the function by providing the expected inputs.

```
multiply(2, 3);
//6
```

Functions have the type `'function'`.

```
typeof multiply
//'function'
```

Variables

Variables are containers for values. Variables store values.

There are two current ways of declaring them plus one that has become obsolete.

`let` declares a variable that can change, meaning it can be reassigned.

The = symbol is the assignment operator.

```
let number = 1;
number = 2;
//2
```

We may assign a value to a variable at the declaration or we can assign a value to an existing variable. The variable `number` was first assigned with the value 1 and then was reassigned to the number 2.

`const` declares a variable that cannot be reassigned.

```
const number = 1;
number = 2;
//Assignment to constant variable
```

Variables have names. They allow us to refer to values using names.

An identifier is a name. They are used to name variables, functions, properties.

The identifier must start with a letter, an underscore, or the dollar sign ($). Then it can be followed by any of those characters and also digits. We cannot use a digit as the first character in a variable name. There are also reserved words that cannot be used as identifiers like `function` or `boolean`.

Key Notes

- Numbers, strings, booleans, `null`, `undefined` and symbols are primitives. All the other values are objects.
- Objects are collections of key-value pairs. Arrays are collections of values.
- Functions allow us to define a block of code performing a distinct task.
- Primitives and objects are both values.
- Variables hold values and let us to refer values by names.
- The `typeof` operator returns the type of value as a string.

Chapter 02: Numbers

Numbers can be simply represented using the number literal. Here are a few examples.

```
0
1
1.2
99999987654321
```

There are two built-in numeric types in JavaScript, `number` and `bigint`, but most probably you are going to use the first one, the number type.

Number Type

Numbers in JavaScript are stored using the double-precision floating-point standard. This format uses in 64 bits. In other languages, this type is called float or double.

Both integers and decimal numbers are stored using this format.

Decimal numbers are represented using a dot.

```
1.2
123.456789
```

The `typeof` operator returns `'number'` for both integers and decimals.

```
typeof 1
//'number'

typeof 1.2
//'number'
```

`Number.isInteger` checks if a value is an integer.

```
Number.isInteger(1);   //true
Number.isInteger(1.2); //false
Number.isInteger('');  //false
```

We can use the underscore separator in numbers to make them easier to read.

```
1_000_000
```

Arithmetic

The main usage of numbers is calculations. We use several numbers in arithmetic operations like addition or multiplication to compute new numbers. The + symbol is the addition operator. The * symbol is the multiplication operator.

```
1 + 2
//3
```

```
2 * 3
//6
```

Subtraction is done with the (-) operator. The / is the division operator.

The % symbol represents the remainder operation. For example, 3 % 2 gives 1 and 8 % 3 gives 2. This is also referred to as the modulo operator.

The exponentiation operator (**) raises the first operand to the power of the second operand.

```
2**0
//1
```

```
2**1
//2
```

```
2**2
//4
```

Calculations with integers up to 2^{53} are always precise. The Number.MAX_SAFE_INTEGER property returns the largest safe integer 9007199254740991.

The decimal arithmetic is inexact so you need to be aware of that and avoid related issues.

Consider the following equality that is `false`. The triple equal operator (===) is used for equality.

```
0.1 + 0.2 === 0.3;
//false
```

That's because `0.1 + 0.2` makes something like `0.30000000000000004`.

The integer arithmetic is exact so we can use that to avoid the previous issue by writing the decimals as fractions.

```
1/10 + 2/10  === 3/10;
//true
```

This is not a problem with JavaScript. It is a known issue with the double-precision floating-point format. Here is the same result in Elixir when using floats.

```
iex> 0.1 + 0.2
0.30000000000000004
```

Big Integers

As already said calculations with integers are precise up to 2^{53}. Trying to do a computation over this limit may give the wrong result.

```
9007199254740991 + 2
//9007199254740992
```

To represent integer numbers larger than $2^{53} - 1$ we can use big integers. A `bigint` number is created by appending `n` to the end of it.

```
0n
1n
```

The previous addition gives the correct result when done with big integers.

```
9007199254740991n + 2n
//9007199254740993n
```

Operations with the +,*, -, % and ** work as expected, but calculations with fractions are truncated.

```
1n / 2n
//0n
```

```
3n / 2n
```

```
//1n
```

```
4n / 2n
//2n
```

Big integers are not strictly equal to the equivalent number values.

```
1 === 1n
//false
```

Computations with both integers and big integers don't work.

```
1 + 2n
//Cannot mix BigInt and other types, use explicit conversions
```

The `typeof` operators returns `'bigint'` for a big integer.

```
typeof 1n
//'bigint'
```

```
typeof BigInt('1')
//'bigint'
```

Converting to Numbers

Number and BigInt Functions

The `Number` and `BigInt` built-in functions can be used to convert other values to numbers. Don't use the `new` operator when making this conversion.

Below is an example of converting the string `'1.2'` into a number.

```
const noText = '1.2';
```

```
const no = Number(noText);
//1.2
```

```
typeof no;
//'number'
```

Here is an example of converting a string to a `BigInt`.

```
const noText = '9007199254740993';
```

```
const no = BigInt(noText);
```

```
//9007199254740993n
```

```
typeof no;
//'bigint'
```

We can use the `Number` and `BigInt` functions to convert all kinds of values not just strings. We can convert for example dates into numbers. The result of the conversion is the number of milliseconds since 1st of January 1970.

```
const currentDate = new Date();
Number(currentDate);
//1629007658253
```

We can convert boolean values to numbers as well.

```
Number(true); //1
Number(false);//0
BigInt(true); //1n
BigInt(false);//0n
```

parseInt and parseFloat

The `parseInt` and `parseFloat` functions are useful for converting strings into numbers.

The `parseInt` function parses a string and returns an integer. It ignores the spaces before and after the string number. If the first non-space character cannot be converted to a number, it returns `NaN`. If there are several numbers in the string separated by other characters it returns only the first one.

```
Number.parseInt("1")    //1
Number.parseInt("1.2") //1
Number.parseInt("1.2 3 4") //1
Number.parseInt(" 1.2 ") //1
Number.parseInt("1 one") //1
Number.parseInt("1one")  //1
Number.parseInt("one")   //NaN
Number.parseInt("")      //NaN
```

The `parseFloat` function parses a string and returns a decimal number. It ignores spaces before and after the string number. If the first non-spaces cannot be converted to a number it returns NaN. It gets only the first decimal number from the string.

```
Number.parseFloat("1")    //1
Number.parseFloat("1.2") //1.2
Number.parseFloat("1.2 3 4") //1.2
Number.parseFloat(" 1.2 ")    //1.2
Number.parseFloat("1 one")    //1
Number.parseFloat("one") //NaN
Number.parseFloat("")    //NaN
```

The result from converting strings to numbers using the Number utility is sometimes different from the result we get from the Number.parseFloat function. That's because Number tries to convert the whole string to a number while Number.parseFloat tries to find the number in the string.

```
Number("1")    //1
Number("1.2") //1.2
Number("1.2 3 4") //NaN
Number(" 1.2 ") //1.2
Number("1 one") //NaN
Number("one")    //NaN
Number("")       //0
```

Methods

Numbers have methods.

How is that even possible? Are numbers actually objects?

No. Numbers are not objects. JavaScript just tries to make them look as such. To access a method on a number it converts the number to an object, using the new Number() or the new BigInt() built-in constructor functions, and then accesses the method on the newly created object.

Here is an example of accessing the toFixed method on a number.

```
let x = 1.23456;
x.toFixed(2);
//1.23
```

toFixed(n) returns a string representation of the number that has n digits after the decimal separator.

Behind the scenes, a wrapper object is created and the `toFixed` method is accessed on it. Something like this happens.

```
new Number(1.23456).toFixed(2)
```

The `toLocaleString` method returns a string with the localized representation of the number. For example, in the USA, the decimal separator is a dot while the decimal separator is a comma in France.

```
(1.2).toLocaleString('en-US');
//'1.2'
```

```
(1.2).toLocaleString('fr-FR');
//'1,2'
```

All the methods available on numbers are store on the `Number.prototype`. The methods for big integers stay on the `BigInt.prototype` object.

Math Object

On the `Math` object we can find practical functions doing mathematical calculations.

`Math.floor` returns the closest integer less than or equal to a given number.

```
Math.floor(1.3)//1
Math.floor(1.9)//1
```

`Math.ceil` returns the closest integer greater than or equal to a given number.

```
Math.ceil(1.3) //2
Math.ceil(1.9) //2
```

`Math.trunc` returns the integer part of a given number by removing all digits after the decimal separator.

```
Math.trunc(1.3) //1
Math.trunc(1.9) //1
Math.trunc(-1.3) //-1
Math.trunc(-1.9) //-1
```

`Math.min` and `Math.max` returns the minimum or the maximum from any number of arguments.

```
Math.min(1,2) //1
Math.min(5,4,3,2,1) //1
Math.max(1,2) //2
Math.max(5,4,3,2,1) //5
```

`Math.random` returns a random decimal number between 0 and 1.

```
Math.random() //0.2827543419586407
```

The `Math` utility functions work only with numbers. They cannot be used with big integers.

```
Math.max(1, 2n)
//Uncaught TypeError: Cannot convert a BigInt value to a number
```

Special Numbers

The language has three special values considered numbers but with distinct behavior.

Infinity

The `Infinity` and `-Infinity` express the positive and negative infinities. `Infinity + 1` results in `Infinity`. `-Infinity - 1` gives `-Infinity`.

`Infinity - Infinity` results in `NaN`.

NaN

In JavaScript, invalid numbers are represented using the `NaN` value. `NaN` and `Number.NaN` both represent the same value.

Even if is called "Not-A-Number" is actually a number. A better name would have been Not-A-Valid-Number.

```
typeof NaN
//'number'
```

`NaN` is not equal to itself. This can be a little strange. It is the only value in the language not equal to itself.

```
NaN === NaN
//false
```

That implies that a variable storing the `NaN` value is not equal to itself.

```
const x = NaN;

x === x
//false
```

Invalid conversions result in NaN.

The `Number` function can convert any value into a number. When it fails to do so it returns NaN. Below are a few examples.

```
Number(null);        //0
Number(undefined);   //NaN
Number('one');       //NaN
Number('2 one');     //NaN
Number(undefined);   //NaN
```

As you can see, converting the **undefined** value and the string **"one"** into a number fails and the result is NaN, the invalid number.

Parsing an invalid string using `Number.parseInt` and `Number.parseFloat` result in NaN.

```
Number.parseInt("");        //NaN
Number.parseInt("one");     //NaN
Number.parseInt("one1");    //NaN
Number.parseFloat("two");   //NaN
```

Invalid arithmetic like trying to get the square root of a negative number, or dividing 0 by 0 results in NaN.

```
Math.sqrt(-1)
//NaN

0/0
//NaN
```

Trying to subtract a string from a number, or mathematical operations with NaN return NaN.

```
1 - "one"
//NaN

1 + undefined
//NaN
```

```
1 * NaN
//NaN
```

isNaN gives false positives.

The global function isNaN tries first to convert the input value to a number and then tells if it is NaN. This approach gives false positives. For example, the string "one" cannot be converted to a number. For this reason, isNaN says that "one" is NaN which is not correct.

```
isNaN(0);
//false

isNaN(undefined));
//true

isNaN('one'));
//true
```

Number.isNaN can correctly check for NaN.

To avoid these issues use the Number.isNaN utility from the Number object.

```
Number.isNaN(0);
//false

Number.isNaN(undefined);
//false

Number.isNaN('one');
//false
```

Key Notes

- JavaScript has two numeric types, number and bigint.
- Integer arithmetic is precise up to a limit (2^{53}).
- Decimal arithmetic is inexact.
- Numbers have methods.
- The `Number` and `BigInt` functions can convert values of any type to numbers.
- Invalid arithmetic operations do not throw exceptions but the result is `NaN`.
- `Number.parseInt` and `Number.parseFloat` utility functions convert strings into numbers.
- The `Math` object contains utility functions for doing mathematical computations with numbers.

Chapter 03: Strings

Strings express text data. Here are a few examples.

```
"Fire cannot kill a dragon"
'Chaos is a ladder'
`Fear cuts deeper than swords`
```

String Literal

Strings can be defined with both single and double quotes.

```
"text"
'text'
```

They both create practically the same string.

```
"text" === 'text'
//true
```

Such a string must fit a single line. We cannot define a string spanning multiple lines this way.

When the string is defined with double quotes we need to escape other double quotes inside it. The \ (backslash) is used for escaping characters.

```
"text with \"double quotes\" inside"
```

However, we don't need to escape single quotes.

```
"text with single 'quotes' "
```

When defining a string with single quotes, the double quotes don't need to be escaped.

```
'text with "double quotes" inside'
```

Two strings containing the same text are equal.

```
"Text" === "Text"
//true
```

The \ (backslash) is also used to include the \ character or a new line in a string. To include a new line in single quoted or double quoted strings use the \n escape sequence.

```
"The first line\nThe second line"
```

Converting to Strings

We can use the `String` built-in function to convert any type of value into a string. It is the best option for converting primitive types into strings. Check the next examples:

```
String(0)
//'0'
```

```
String(true)
//'true'
```

```
String(null)
//'null'
```

```
String(undefined)
//'undefined'
```

```
String([1,2,3])
//'1,2,3'
```

```
String({ msg: 'Hi'})
//'[object Object]'
```

```
String(Symbol('id'))
//'Symbol(id)'
```

As you can see all conversions look fine except for the object which was transformed into a raw generic string `'[object Object]'`. Even the array is converted into a nice string with all its values separated by commas.

Methods

JavaScript allows us to call methods on strings giving the illusion they are some kind of objects. Strings are not objects. When we call a method on a string JavaScript creates a wrapper object using the built-in `String` constructor and calls that method on the newly created object.

For example, calling the `trim` method on a string looks something like this behind the scenes.

```
new String(" text ").trim();
```

The `trim` method removes whitespace before the start and after the end of a string. All whitespace characters are removed including spaces, tabs, newlines.

```
const text = " \t\ntext\n\t ";
const newText = text.trim();
//"text"
```

All string methods are defined on the `String.prototype` object.

Immutability

Strings are immutable, once declared strings cannot be changed. None of the string methods can change the source strings. They always create a new text.

Consider the next example. The `replace` method does not change the current string but creates a new one.

The `replace` method searches a string for a specified substring and returns a new string where the given substring is replaced. It replaces only the first occurrence when called with a string as the first argument.

```
const str = "abc";

const newStr = str.replace("a", "A");

console.log(str);
//"abc"

console.log(newStr)
//"Abc"
```

Characters in a string can be access like in an array using an index inside brackets. This may give the impression that we can change the character at that index. This is a false assumption. Characters in a string cannot be changed.

```
const text = 'ABC';
text[0] = 'X';
//Cannot assign to read only property '0' of string 'ABC'
```

Other languages have a special type for a single character usually called char. There is no such type in JavaScript. To represent a character simply use a string storing that single character.

Searching

Methods allow detecting if a substring is contained in a string.

The `indexOf` method returns the index of the first occurrence of a specified text in a string. When the text is not found it returns -1.

```
const quote = "Here we stand";

const firstIndex = quote.indexOf(" ");
//4
```

The `lastIndexOf` method returns the index of the last occurrence of a specified text in a string. When the text is not found it returns -1.

```
const quote = "Here we stand";

const lastIndex = quote.lastIndexOf(" ");
//7
```

The `startsWith` method checks if a string begins with the given substring and returns a boolean (true/false).

```
const quote = "First in Battle";
quote.startsWith("First")
//true
```

The `endsWith` method checks if a string ends with the given substring and returns true or false as appropriate.

```
const quote = "We Remember";
quote.endsWith("We")
//false
```

The `includes` method checks if a string contains a given substring and returns `true` or `false` as appropriate.

```
const quote = "Our Blades are Sharp";
quote.includes("are")
//true
```

Extracting

There are three methods, maybe too many, for extracting a part of a string.

The `substr(start, length)` method extracts part of a string, beginning at the specified index and returning the specified number of characters. The first character is at the index 0.

```
const quote = "Winter is coming";

const part1 = quote.substr(0, 6);
//Winter

const part2 = quote.substr(10, 6);
//coming
```

The `start` index is required but the `length` is optional. If omitted it extracts the rest of the string.

```
const quote = "Winter is coming";

const part = quote.substr(6);
// is coming
```

The `substring(start, end)` method returns the part of a string between the `start` and `end` indexes. It begins with the character at the `start` index and ends but does not include the character at the `end` index.

```
const quote = "We Stand Together";

const part = quote.substring(3, 8);
// Stand
```

If the `end` index is omitted it extracts till the end of the string.

```
const quote = "We Stand Together";
```

```
const part = quote.substring(3);
// Stand Together
```

It can be combined with the **indexOf** method. Consider the following code extracting the text after the first comma.

```
const quote = "You know nothing,Jon Snow";
```

```
const commaIndex = quote.indexOf(",");
```

```
const part = quote.substring(commaIndex + 1);
//"Jon Snow"
```

slice has the same interface as **substring** and was added basically to imitate the array interface.

Concatenating

The + operator does both addition and concatenation.

When one of the operands is a string, the plus operator (+) becomes the concatenation operator. Check the next examples.

```
"A" + " " + "text"
//"A text"
```

```
1 + "2"
//"12"
```

The **concat** method can achieve similar behavior. It concatenates all the string arguments to the current string and returns a new string.

```
"A".concat("B")
//"AB"
```

```
"A".concat(" ", "text")
//"A text"
```

```
"1".concat(2)
//"12"
```

Converting to an Array

The `split` method splits a text into an array of substrings based on a separator. Below is an example.

```
const quote = 'Winter is coming';
const words = quote.split(' ');
//["Winter", "is", "coming"]
```

Here is another example of splitting a text using a comma as the separator.

```
const csv = 'Fire,and,Blood';
const arr = csv.split(',');
//["Fire", "and", "Blood"]
```

Template Strings

Template strings literals can create strings that span multiple lines and that allow interpolation.

Template strings are defined using the backtick (`` ` ``) character.

```
`Wisdom
 and
 Strength`
```

Valid expressions can be placed inside template string literals. The expressions are evaluated and converted into strings.

```
const word = "Awake";
`${word}! ${word}!`
//"Awake! Awake!"
```

Unicode UTF-16

JavaScript uses 16 bits to represent a string element meaning it can express up to 2^{16} different characters. Most of the common characters, including all English letters fit in 16 bits, but some characters, such as an emoji, take up two code units in a string.

A character is stored using one or two UTF-16 code units.

The `length` property is said to return the number of characters in a string, but it actually returns the number of UTF-16 units. It returns the number of characters only if each character fits in 16 bits otherwise it returns a large number.

```
const word = 'Hi';

console.log(word.length)
//2
```

Consider the next example showing the emoji character that requires 2 x 16 bits to be stored.

```
const word = 'Hi☺';
console.log(word.length)
//4
```

As you can see the `length` property does not correctly says the number of characters in this case.

The `charAt` method returns a new string containing a single UTF-16 code unit located at the given index. It makes it clear that we can only read the code unit at a specific index.

```
const word = 'Hi;
console.log(word.charAt(0))
//H
```

However, the `charAt` does not return the emoji character correctly because it uses 2 code units.

```
const word = 'Hi☺';
console.log(word.charAt(2))
//�
```

To have the correct size and index access in this case we need to convert the strings to an array of characters.

Be aware that `split` method does not correctly transform a string into an array of characters when using an empty string as a separator.

```
const word = 'Hi☺';
const chars = word.split("");
//["H", "i", "�", "�"]
```

The `Array.from` utility creates a new array from an array-like or iterable object.

An array-like object is one that has index access and the `length` property, but none of the array methods. A string is an array-like object.

`Array.from` handles the case when the characters take more than 16-bit. Once we have the array of chars we can use the `chars.length` to correctly count the numbers of characters in a string.

```
const word = 'Hi☺';
const chars = Array.from(word);

console.log(word.length);
//4
console.log(chars.length);
//3
```

When the string is transformed correctly into an array of characters we can access accurately the character at a given index even if takes two code units to be represented.

```
console.log(chars[2]);
//☺
```

Key Notes

- Strings can be created using single quotes, double quotes or with backticks.
- Strings are immutable.
- Strings look like they have methods.
- The built-in `String` function can convert any value into a string.
- The + operator does both addition and concatenation.
- Methods can detect if a substring is contained in a string.
- Methods allow extracting part of a string.
- Strings can be converted to and from an array.
- The template strings can span multiple lines and allow interpolation.
- Strings are represented using Unicode UTF-16.

Chapter 04: Booleans

The boolean type has two values `true` and `false`.

We can use the `typeof` operator to find the type of these values.

```
typeof false //boolean
typeof true  //boolean
```

Comparison Operators

The comparison operators compare two operands and return a boolean.

The `===` is the equality operator and `!==` is the not equal operator.

```
1 === 1
//true
```

```
1 !== 2
//true
```

The `<` operator evaluates to `true` if the first operand is less than the second operand. Otherwise, it returns `false`.

```
1 < 2  //true
2 < 2  /false
```

The `<=` is the less or equal operator.

```
2 <= 2 //true
```

The `>` operator evaluates to `true` if the first operand is greater than the second operand. Otherwise, it returns `false`.

```
3 > 2   //true
2 > 2   //false
```

The >= is the greater or equal operator.

```
2 >= 2  //true
```

Truthy and Falsy

In JavaScript, all values are either truthy or falsy.

`false`, `null`, `undefined`, `NaN`, `0`, `0n` and `''` are falsy values. All the other values are truthy.

It means that we can put a test condition using any kind of value.

The conditional operator (also called ternary operator) evaluates the value on the left side of the question mark and when it is truthy returns the middle value otherwise it returns the value on the right side of the colon.

```
const value = true;
console.log(value ? 'True' : 'False');
//'True'
```

Below is an example of using the conditional operator having a condition over a string.

```
const value = '';
console.log(value ? 'Truthy' : 'Falsy');
//'Falsy'
```

Logical Operators

There are three logical operators: And, Or, and Not. The && symbol represents the And operator. || is the Or operator. The Not operator is as an exclamation mark (!).

Not Operator

The Not operator (!) negates an expression.

When the operand is falsy Not (!) returns `true`. When the operand is truthy it returns `false`.

The Not operator works on a single operand and returns a boolean. Here are a few examples.

```
!false //true
!true  //false
```

```
!undefined //true
!null  //true
!0  //true
!1  //false
!{} //false
![] //false
!'' //true
!'text' //false
```

Or Operator

When the first operand is truthy OR (||) returns the first operand and the second is not evaluated. When the first operand is falsy then it returns the second operand.

```
const value = null;
```

```
const isNullish = value === null || value === undefined;
//true
```

And Operator

When the first operand is falsy the And (&&) operator returns the first operand and the second operand is not evaluated. When the first operand is truthy, then it returns the second operand.

```
const value = 1;
```

```
const isNotNullish = value !== null && value !== undefined;
//true
```

There are a pair of mathematical transformation rules called De Morgan's Laws that can be helpful.

- not (A or B) = (not A) and (not B)
- not (A and B) = (not A) or (not B)

In JavaScript, these laws can be written like this.

```
!(a || b) === !a && !b;
```

```
!(a && b) === !a || !b;
```

Consider our previous example checking if a value is nullish.

```
value === null || value === undefined
```

The following two expressions are both valid and equivalent for checking if a value is not nullish.

```
!(value === null || value === undefined)
  === !(value === null) && !(value === undefined);
```

Converting to Booleans

We can convert all values to booleans using the `Boolean` built-in function.

Truthy values are converted to `true`. Falsy values are converted to `false`.

Below are a few examples.

```
Boolean(undefined); //false
Boolean(null); //false
Boolean(0);  //false
Boolean(1);  //true
Boolean({}); //true
Boolean([]); //true
Boolean(''); //false
Boolean('text'); //true
```

Double Negation

Applying a double negation converts any value to a boolean.

Using the Not operator (`!`) on a falsy value results in the `true` boolean value. Applying again the Not operator to the `true` value returns `false`.

In a similar way applying twice the Not operator (`!`) on a truthy value returns `true`.

As you guess, we can use a double negation to transform any value into a boolean.

```
!!undefined //false
!!null //false
!!0  //false
!!1  //true
!!{} //true
!![] //true
!!'' //false
```

However, using the `Boolean` function is preferable. It makes the conversion clearer.

Key Notes

- The boolean type has two values `true` and `false`.
- `false`, `null`, `undefined`, `NaN`, `0`, `On`, and `''` are falsy values. All the other values are truthy.
- The And (`&&`) and Or(`||`) return one of the operands.
- The Not (`!`) operator negates an expression and returns a boolean.
- The `Boolean` function converts any value to a boolean.
- Applying a double negation converts any value to a boolean.

Chapter 05: Objects

Objects in JavaScript are different compared to what they are in other languages. They look more like maps.

The object literal is the simplest way to create an object. We define a set of properties inside curly braces {} separated by commas. Below is an example.

```
const product = {
  name: 'apple',
  category: 'fruits',
  price: 1.99
}
```

The previous object has three properties. The first property has the key `name` and the string value `"apple"`.

Properties

Dynamic Collections

Objects are unordered dynamic collections of properties.

Once an object is created we can add, edit or delete properties from it. Below is a case of adding and deleting the `category` property to/from the previous `product` object.

Both adding and editing are done in the same way. If the property already exists it is changed otherwise it is added.

```
const product = {
  name: 'kiwi',
}
```

```
product.category = 'fruits';
//{name: "kiwi", category: "fruits"}
```

Deletion is done using the `delete` operator.

```
delete product.category;
//{name: "kiwi"}
```

Accessing Properties

Properties can be accessed using the dot and the bracket notations.

When the key is a valid identifier we can use the dot notation.

```
product.name
//"kiwi"
```

When the key is not a valid identifier we need to define the key as a string and use the bracket notation for accessing the property.

```
const product = {
   "english name" : "papaya"
}
```

```
product["english name"]
//"papaya"
```

Property Keys

The property key is a string and has to be unique in the collection. When non-string values are used as keys they are converted to strings. Look what happens when we try to use another object as a key.

```
const product = {
   name: 'lemon',
   category: 'fruits',
}
```

```
const categoryKey = {
   toString(){
      return 'fruits'
   }
}
```

```
game[categoryKey];
//"fruits"
```

When the `categoryKey` is used as a key it is first converted to a string using the `toString` method, then the result `'category'` string key is used to retrieve the value. The previous code gives the same result as `product['category']`.

Shorthand Property Names

Consider the case where we have the values of our properties stored in variables.

```
const name = 'apple';
const category = 'fruits';
const price = 1.99;

const product = {
  name: name,
  category: category,
  price: price
}
```

JavaScript supports what is called the shorthand property names. It allows us to create an object using just the name of the variable. It builds a property with the same name. The next object literal is equivalent to the previous one.

```
const name = 'apple';
const category = 'fruits';
const price = 1.99;

const product = {
  name,
  category,
  price
}
```

Property Values

The value of a property can a primitive, an object, or a function.

Objects can store other objects. Consider the next case where the `nutrients` property holds an object.

```
const product = {
  name: 'apple',
  category: 'fruits',
  price: 1.99,
  nutrients : {
    carbs: 0.95,
    fats: 0.3,
    protein: 0.2
  }
}
```

Here is how we can access the `carbs` property.

```
product.nutrients.carbs
//0.95
```

Objects can store functions.

The following object has the property `toString` storing a function.

```
const product = {
  name : 'papaya',
  toString: function(){
    return this.name;
  }
};


product.toString();
//"papaya"
```

this

When a function is stored on an object it can be used as a method. Notice that inside methods we can use the `this` keyword to access properties on the associated object.

Remember that functions are independent units of behavior in JavaScript. They are not necessarily part of an object.

When functions are part of an object they become methods and they need a way to access other members on the object. `this` is the function context and gives access to properties on the same object.

Hash Maps

An object in JavaScript is similar to what in other languages is called a map, a hash map, an associative array, or a dictionary.

Because keys are strings we can say that objects map strings to values.

Keys have an O(1) access time.

O(1) means that it takes a constant time to access the key, no matter the amount of data on the map.

O(n) means it takes an amount of time linear with the size of the list. The larger the list the bigger the time access.

This is why you may see objects used as maps to search for unique keys.

```
const productsMap = {
  1 : { name: 'apple'},
  2 : { name: 'kiwi'},
  3 : { name: 'papaya'}
}
```

Now we can use the productsMap to get a product object by id in a constant time O(1) without looping through the list.

Object Utilities

Object.freeze

Object.freeze freezes an object. A frozen object cannot be changed anymore. It returns the same object that was passed in.

This is the simplest way to achieve immutability by freezing the object at creation.

```
const product = Object.freeze({
  name: 'lemon',
});

product.category = 'fruits';
//Cannot add property category, object is not extensible

product.name = "orange";
//Cannot assign to read only property 'name' of object
```

The only thing to note is that `Object.freeze` freezes only the immediate properties of an object doing what is called a "shallow freeze".

Object.isFrozen

`Object.isFrozen` detects if an object is frozen.

```
Object.isFrozen(product)
//true
```

Object.keys

`Object.keys` gives an array with all the owned property keys. Check the code below retrieving all the keys of the `product` object into a new array of strings.

```
const product = {
  name : 'pineapple',
  category: 'fruits',
  toString: function(){
    return this.name;
  }
};

const keys = Object.keys(product);
//["name", "category", "toString"]
```

Once we have the array of keys we can start using the array methods.

Object.values

`Object.values` returns an array with all the owned property values.

```
const values = Object.values(product);
//["pineapple", "fruits", f]
```

Object.entries

`Object.entries` returns an array of `[key, value]` pairs representing all the owned properties of an object.

```
const product = {
  name : 'pineapple',
  category: 'fruits',
```

```
  toString: function(){
    return this.name;
  }
};

const keyValuePairs = Object.entries(product);
//[
//["name", "pineapple"],
//["category", "fruits"],
//["toString", f]
//]
```

Notice that an entry is an array with two values [key, value].

Object.fromEntries

We can do the reverse operation and transform an array of [key, value] pairs into an object using the Object.fromEntries utility. Consider the code below.

```
const keyValuePairs = [
  ["name", "pineapple"],
  ["category", "fruits"],
]

const product = Object.fromEntries(keyValuePairs);
//{name: "pineapple", category: "fruits"}
```

Object.defineProperty

The Object.defineProperty utility modifies an existing property or defines a new one on an object. It changes and returns the modified object.

Object.defineProperty is mainly used to set specific property descriptors like enumerability or defining a read-only property.

Consider the previous product object.

```
const product = {
  name : 'pineapple',
  category: 'fruits',
  toString: function(){
```

```
      return this.name;
  }
};
```

```
const keys = Object.keys(product);
//["name", "category", "toString"]
```

By default all new properties are enumerable. As you can see the `toString` property name is returned when calling the `Object.key` utility.

If we don't want `toString` to be an enumerable property we can mark it as such using the `Object.defineProperty` utility.

```
Object.defineProperty(product, 'toString', {
  enumerable: false
});
```

```
const keys = Object.keys(product);
//["name", "category"]
```

Nonetheless, we can still change the `toString` property if we want.

```
product.toString = undefined;
```

We can avoid such behavior by setting the writable descriptor on the `toString` property as `false`.

```
'use strict';
//...
```

```
Object.defineProperty(product, 'toString', {
    enumerable: false,
    writable: false
});
```

```
product.toString = undefined;
//Cannot assign to read only property 'toString' of object
```

The `Object.defineProperty` utility can be used to add dynamic getters and setters. Below is an example of adding a dynamic getter to the product object. The getter returns the value of the property only if the user has access otherwise it throws an error.

```
const product = {
  name: 'peach',
```

```
  category: 'fruits',
};

const hasRight = false;
const propName = 'name';

Object.defineProperty(product, propName, {
  get : function () {
    if(hasRight){
      return product[propName];
    } else {
      throw `${propName} no access`;
    }
  }
});

console.log(product.name)
//name no access
```

Object.assign

`Object.assign` copies the owned properties from one or more source objects to a target object. It returns the target object.

Below is an example where we copy the properties from the `productMethods` object into the `product` object.

```
const productMethods = {
  toString: function(){
    return this.name;
  }
};

const product = {
  name: 'blueberry',
  category: 'fruits'
};

Object.assign(product, productMethods);
product.toString()
//'blueberry'
```

We can avoid modifying the exiting `product` object and instead create a new object containing properties from both the exiting `product` and `productMethods` objects. We do that by copying their properties to an empty object (`{}`).

```
const newProduct = Object.assign({}, product, productMethods);
```

```
newProduct.toString()
//'blueberry'
```

As you guessed `Object.assign` can be useful for cloning objects.

```
const product = {
  name: 'lime'
};
```

```
const newProduct = Object.assign({}, product);
//{name: "lime"}
```

```
product === newProduct
//false
```

Key Notes

- The object literal is the simplest way for creating an object.
- Objects are unordered dynamic collections of properties. The property keys are converted to strings.
- Properties can be accessed using the dot and the bracket notations.
- Objects can store functions and other objects.
- Objects are more like hash maps.
- `Object.freeze` and `Object.isFrozen` allow freezing and detecting frozen objects.
- `Object.keys`, `Object.values` and `Object.entries` help us to extract all the owned properties of an object in a new array giving access to the array methods.
- Transforming objects into an array of `[key, value]` pairs and then back into objects becomes straightforward using the `Object.entries` and `Object.fromEntries` helpers.
- `Object.assign` helps to clone objects or copying the properties of several objects into a new one.

Chapter 06: Prototypes

In JavaScript, objects inherit from other objects. Objects have a hidden property called `__proto__` pointing to their prototype. Most objects inherit from the global `Object.prototype`.

```
const product = {
  name: 'lime'
}
```

```
product.__proto__ === Object.prototype;
//true
```

The `product` object has properties like `toString` or `toLocaleString` even if we haven't defined such methods. They are inherited from the `Object.prototype` object.

```
console.log(product.toString);
//f toString() { [native code] }
```

```
console.log(product.toLocaleString);
//f toLocaleString() { [native code] }
```

Object.create

JavaScript has what is called the prototype system that allows sharing behavior between objects. The main idea is to create an object called the prototype with the common behavior and then use it to build new objects.

The prototype system allows creating objects that inherit behavior from other objects.

The prototype is usually used to store methods, not data. Let's create a prototype object that allows us to add products and get the total price

55

from a shopping cart.

```
const cartPrototype = {
  addProduct: function(product){
    if(!this.products){
      this.products = [product]
    } else {
      this.products.push(product);
    }
  },
  getTotalPrice: function(){
    return this.products
      .reduce((total, p) => total + p.price, 0);
  }
}
```

The value of the addProduct property is a function and uses the special this keyword to access and modify other properties on the object.

We can also write the previous methods using the shorthand notation.

```
const cartPrototype = {
  addProduct(product){ },
  getTotalPrice(){ }
}
```

The cartPrototype is the prototype object that keeps the common behavior in two methods addProduct and getTotalPrice.

The Object.create utility buils a new object inheriting behavior from the given prototype.

```
const cart = Object.create(cartPrototype);
cart.addProduct({name: 'orange', price: 1.25});
cart.addProduct({name: 'lemon', price: 1.75});

cart.getTotalPrice();
//3
```

The cartPrototype object is the prototype of the cart object. cart has a hidden property called __proto__ that points to this prototype object.

```
cart.__proto__ === cartPrototype;
//true
```

When we use a method on an object, that method is first searched on the object itself then on its prototype.

Object.getPrototypeOf

Even if we can access the prototype of an object with the __proto__ property the better approach is to use the Object.getPrototypeOf utility function.

```
Object.getPrototypeOf(cart) === cartPrototype;
//true
```

Even the empty object literal has a prototype, the Object.prototype.

```
const obj = {};

Object.getPrototypeOf(obj) === Object.prototype;
//true
```

Data on Prototypes

You may wonder why we haven't defined and initialized the products property on the prototype object itself.

We shouldn't do that. Prototypes should be used to share behavior, not data. Sharing data will lead to having the same products on several cart objects. Consider the code below.

```
const cartPrototype = {
  products:[],
  addProduct: function(product){
      this.products.push(product);
  },
  getTotalPrice: function(){}
}

const cart1 = Object.create(cartPrototype);
cart1.addProduct({name: 'orange', price: 1.25});
cart1.addProduct({name: 'lemon', price: 1.75});

cart1.getTotalPrice();
//3
```

```
const cart2 = Object.create(cartPrototype);
cart2.getTotalPrice();
//3
```

Both `cart1` and `cart2` objects inheriting the common behavior from the `cartPrototype` also share the same data. We don't want that. Prototypes should be used to share behavior, not data.

Changing Objects

Changes are done on the current object, not on its prototype. Prototypes are used for reading only.

When adding, editing, or deleting a property that is done on the current object.

For example, the `Object.prototype` has the `toString` property. Consider the empty object inheriting from `Object.prototype`. The `delete` operator in the following example does nothing, it does not delete the `toString` property from the prototype.

```
const obj = {};
console.log(obj.toString);
//f toString() { [native code] }

delete obj.toString
console.log(obj.toString);
//f toString() { [native code] }
```

When we change the `toString` property, a new property is added to the current object, the prototype is not changed. At this point, both the current object and the prototype have a property with the same name. The one from the current object is used.

```
const obj = {};
obj.toString = function(){};
```

Freezing Prototypes

Prototypes can be frozen.

When the prototype is frozen the object inheriting from it cannot have new properties with the same names. Consider the following frozen prototype.

```
const prototype = Object.freeze({
```

```
  toString : function (){
    return this.name;
  }
});
```

Because the prototype is frozen and has the **toString** property we cannot define a property with the same name on the new object inheriting from it.

```
const product = Object.create(prototype);

product.name = 'lime';
product.toString = function (){
    return `Name: ${this.name}`;
  };
//Cannot assign to read only property 'toString' of object
```

Object.assign vs Object.create

As you have seen we were able to add the **toString** method to the **product** object with both the `Object.assign` and `Object.create`. The difference is that `Object.assign` adds the property to each newly created object.

```
const prototype = {
  toString : function (){
    return this.name;
  }
};

const product = Object.assign({ name: 'lemon'}, prototype);
product.toString();
//'lemon'
```

`Object.create` adds only a reference to the existing prototype on the newly created objects. It doesn't copy all the reusable properties. This difference can be noticed only when building thousands of objects.

```
const product = Object.create(prototype);
product.name = 'lemon';

product.toString();
//'lemon'
```

Classes

The prototype system is not a common way of creating objects. Developers are more familiar with building objects out of classes.

The class syntax allows a more familiar way of creating objects sharing a common behavior. It still creates the same prototype behind the scene but the syntax is more clear and we also avoid the previous data-related issue. The class offers a special function to define the data distinct for each object called the constructor.

Here is the same cart object built using the class sugar syntax.

```
class Cart{
  constructor(){
    this.products = [];
  }

  addProduct(product){
    this.products.push(product);
  }

  getTotalPrice(){
    return this.products
      .reduce((total, p) => total + p.price, 0);
  }
}

const cart = new Cart();
cart.addProduct({name: 'orange', price: 1.25});
cart.addProduct({name: 'lemon', price: 1.75});

console.log(cart.getTotalPrice());
//3

const cart2 = new Cart();
console.log(cart2.getTotalPrice());
//0
```

Notice that the class has a constructor method that initialized distinct data for each new object. The data in the constructor is not shared between instances. In order to create a new instance, we use the **new** keyword.

The class syntax is more clear and familiar to most developers. Nevertheless, it does a similar thing, it creates a prototype with all the methods and uses it to define new objects. The prototype can be accessed with `Cart.prototype`.

```
Object.getPrototypeOf(cart) === Cart.prototype;
//true
```

It turns out that the prototype system is flexible enough to allow the class syntax. So the class system can be emulated using the prototype system.

Private Properties

The only thing is that the **products** property on the new object is public by default.

```
console.log(cart.products);
//[{name: "orange", price: 1.25}
// {name: "lemon", price: 1.75}]
```

We can make it private using the hash # prefix.

Private properties are declared with **#name** syntax. **#** is a part of the property name itself and should be used for declaring and accessing the property. Here is an example of declaring **products** as a private property.

```
class Cart{
  #products

  constructor(){
    this.#products = [];
  }

  addProduct(product){
    this.#products.push(product);
  }

  getTotalPrice(){
    return this.#products
      .reduce((total, p) => total + p.price, 0);
  }
}

cart.#products;
```

```
//Private field '#products'
//must be declared in an enclosing class
```

Extending the Array

The extends keyword in the class declarations creates a class that is a child of another class.

Here is an example of extending the Array class and adding a simple new method returning the first element.

```
class ExtendedArray extends Array {
  first() {
    return this[0];
  }
}
```

Behind the scene, the ExtendedArray.prototype is created containing the new method and inheriting from the Array.prototype.

The Array.of method creates a new Array instance containing all the passed arguments. For example below we can see how to create an array containing the 1, 2, and 3 values.

```
const arr = Array.of(1, 2, 3);
//[1, 2, 3]
```

In a similar way, we can use the ExtendedArray.of method on the new class to create a new array that supports also the first method.

```
const arr = ExtendedArray.of(1, 2, 3);
//ExtendedArray(3) [1, 2, 3]
```

Now are able to call the first method on the new extended array.

```
arr.first();
//1
```

If we inspect the new object, we can notice that the "hidden" __proto__ property points to ExtendArray.prototype, which also has the __proto__ property referring the Array.prototype.

Invoking Standard Methods

The question is what kind of arrays are returned when using the standard array methods like map or filter.

Consider a trivial mapping function doubling a number.

```
function double(no){
  return no * 2;
}
```

Here is the result of calling the `map` method on an extended array. It returns a new extended array.

```
const newArr = arr.map(double);
//ExtendedArray(3) [2, 4, 6]
```

On the new extended array, we are able to call the `first` method.

```
newArr.first();
//2
```

Key Notes

- Objects inherit from other objects.
- Changes are done on the current object, not on its prototype.
- `Object.create` buils a new object inheriting from an existing prototype.
- `Object.getPrototypeOf` returns the prototype of a given object.
- The `class` keyword creates the illusion of a class-based language, but it is not. Class is sugar syntax over the prototype system.
- The `extends` keyword allows creating a class as a child of another class. The `Array` can be extended with new methods this way.

Chapter 07: Symbols

Symbols are primitive values created with the `Symbol` function.

Below are two examples.

```
Symbol()
Symbol('name')
```

The `Symbol` function accepts an optional description text but it creates a unique value each time it is invoked even if it is called with the same description.

```
Symbol('add_todo') === Symbol('add_todo')
//false
```

The `typeof` operator returns `'symbol'`.

```
typeof Symbol()
//'symbol'

typeof Symbol('name')
//'symbol'
```

Property Keys

I said that property keys are strings, which is mostly the case, but keys can also be symbols.

Here is an example of using a symbol as a key.

```
const titleSym = Symbol('title')
const book = {
 [titleSym] : 'JavaScript the Good Parts'
}
```

```
console.log(book)
// {Symbol(title): "JavaScript the Good Parts"}
```

We can retrieve the associated value by providing the same symbol key.

```
console.log(book[titleSym]);
//JavaScript the Good Parts
```

When defining properties using symbols, if these symbols are not shared, other parts of the code are not able to properly access these properties.

```
console.log(book.title);
//undefined
```

```
console.log(book[Symbol('title')]);
//undefined
```

Nonetheless, we can use `Object.getOwnPropertySymbols`. It returns an array with all the symbols used as property keys.

Once we have that array we can use it to access the symbol properties.

```
const symbols = Object.getOwnPropertySymbols(book);
const sym = symbols[0];

console.log(book[sym]);
//'JavaScript the Good Parts'
```

Shared Symbols

The `Symbol` function does not create a global symbol available in the entire application. However, we can build global symbols using the `Symbol.for` utility.

The `Symbol.for(key)` helper searches for the symbol with the given key in the global symbol registry and returns it when found. Otherwise, a new symbol is created in the global symbol registry with that key.

```
Symbol.for('name') === Symbol.for('name'));
//true
```

The `Symbol.keyFor(sym)` helper retrieves the symbol key from the global symbol registry for the given symbol.

```
const nameSym = Symbol.for('name');
```

```
const key = Symbol.keyFor(nameSym);
//'name'
```

Symbols build with the `Symbol` function are local and not added to the global symbol registry. Searching for such a key returns `undefined`.

```
const sym = Symbol('name');
const key = Symbol.keyFor(sym);
//undefined
```

Type Conversions

Symbols cannot be converted into numbers. Trying to do so throws an error.

```
Number(Symbol(''))
//TypeError: Cannot convert a Symbol value to a number
```

Symbols can be transformed into strings using the `String` function.

```
String(Symbol())
//'Symbol()'
```

Nonetheless, symbols are not automatically converted into strings. Consider the following use cases trying to concatenate a symbol to a string.

```
'1' + Symbol()
//TypeError: Cannot convert a Symbol value to a string
```

```
'1'.concat(Symbol())
//TypeError: Cannot convert a Symbol value to a string
```

String Representation

The `toString` method returns the string representation of a symbol.

```
const symbol = Symbol();
symbol.toString();
//'Symbol()'
```

The string representation contains also the name passed as an argument to the `Symbol` function.

```
const symbol = Symbol('add_todo');
symbol.toString();
//'Symbol(add_todo)'
```

The key is included in the string representation also when using `Symbol.for` to create or reuse a symbol.

```
const symbol = Symbol.for('add_todo');
console.log(symbol.toString());
//'Symbol(add_todo)'
```

Key Notes

- `Symbol(desc)` builds a new unique symbol primitive each time is called.
- Symbols can be created in a global registry and shared with other parts of the code using the `Symbol.for` utility.
- Symbols can be used as keys on objects.
- Symbols are not automatically converted into strings. We need to do an explicit conversion if want that transformation to happen.

Chapter 08: Functions

Functions are one of the most powerful features in JavaScript. There are three ways we can create a function: the function declaration, the function expression, and the arrow syntax.

Function Declaration

The function declaration starts with the `function` keyword that must be the first keyword on that line. Then the name of the function follows along with the input parameters. The function body is defined inside curly braces. Functions usually return a value. The return value stays after the `return` statement.

Note that the return statement stops the execution of the function.

```
function sum(x, y){
  return x + y;
}
```

Function Expressions

When the `function` keyword is not the first on the line we create function expressions. The name is optional in this case. There can be anonymous function expressions or named function expressions.

```
const sum = function(x, y){
  return x + y;
}
```

Function expressions need to be first defined and then they can be invoked.

Arrow Functions

The arrow syntax is a compact alternative to defining a function expression.

There is no `function` keyword this time just the list of parameters wrapped inside parathesis, followed by the arrow symbol `=>` and the expression doing the computation.

When there is only a single input there is no need to use parentheses around the parameter.

```
const identity = x => x;
```

When there are at least two input parameters they are surrounded by parathesis.

```
const sum = (x, y) => x + y;
```

Returning an object requires wrapping it in parenthesis.

```
const createCounter = count => ({ count });
createCounter(0);
//{count: 0}
```

When just returning an expression we don't use the `return` statement in the arrow function definition. Nonetheless, if the function has a block of code we need to wrap it inside curly braces and use the `return` statement to deliver the result. Below is an example.

```
const divide = (no, divisior) => {
  if(divisior === 0){
    throw "Divsion by 0";
  }

  return no / divisior;
}

divide(2, 0);
//Uncaught Divsion by 0

divide(2, 1);
//2
```

Expressions

An expression is a piece of code that produces a value.

Any value is basically in expression. The most common way of writing expression is by using operators. Below are a few examples.

```
1 + 2
7 - 3 - 1
null === undefined
null || 0
!false
```

Functions return values as such they can be used inside expressions.

```
Math.pow(2, 3)
1 + Math.max(1, 3)
```

When defining a small function using the arrow syntax we are usually using an expression after the => sign.

```
const max = (a, b) => a > b ? a : b;
max(1, 2);
//2
```

```
a > b ? a : b
```
is an expression.

Arguments

Functions can be called with any number of arguments.

First, we need to understand the difference between parameters and arguments.

Parameters are the ones used when creating the function with any of the previous forms. Usually, parameters are defined inside parenthesis and are separated by commas. Below is a function with two parameters.

```
function sum(x, y){
    return x + y;
}
```

Arguments are the values used when invoking the function.

```
sum(1, 2);
//3
```

When invoking the function with more arguments than it expects the extra arguments are ignored. Here is an example of calling the previous sum function with three arguments.

```
const total = sum(1, 2, 3);
//3
```

When invoking the function with fewer arguments than it expects the missing parameters are set to undefined. In the following example, the sum function expecting two arguments is called with only one. The second expected parameter is set to undefined. Arithmetic with undefined results in NaN.

```
const total = sum(1);
//NaN
```

Rest Parameter

The rest parameter syntax allows a function to take any number of arguments as an array. The rest parameter is prefixed with three dots (...) followed by the name of the array.

Below is an example.

```
function doSomething(...arr) {
    console.log(arr);
}

doSomething(1, 2, 3);
//[1, 2, 3]
```

There can be only one rest parameter and is the last one in the function definition.

```
function doSomething(a, b, ...arr) {
    console.log(a);
    console.log(b);
    console.log(arr);
}

doSomething(1, 2, 3, 4, 5);
//1
//2
//[3, 4, 5]
```

Function Invocation

In JavaScript, functions can serve various roles and as such can be invoked in several ways.

Invoking as Function

The function invocation is straightforward. We use the function name followed by arguments wrapped inside parenthesis.

Consider the sum function expecting two arguments.

```
function sum(x, y){
   return x + y;
}
```

Here is the function invocation.

```
sum(1, 2);
//3
```

Self-invoking Function

Function expressions can be invoked after creation. These kinds of functions are called IIFE (Immediately Invoked Function Expression).

Here is an example of an IIFE created using an arrow function.

```
(() => {
   console.log("App has started");
})();
//"App has started"
```

Function expressions can be created with the arrow syntax or with the function keyword. In a function expression, the function keyword is not the first on the line.

Here is the same self-executing function rewritten using the function keyword.

```
(function(){
   console.log("App has started");
})();
//"App has started"
```

You may have seen the ! operator used before the **function** keyword and wondered why. This is why. It is used to convert the function into a function expression so that it can be auto executed.

```
!function(){
  console.log("App has started");
}();
//"App has started"
```

Invoking as Method

Functions can be also methods on objects. In this case, we need to use the object reference when calling it. Here is an example of invoking a method on an object.

```
const counter = {
  count : 0,
  increment(){
    this.count += 1;
    return this.count;
  }
}

counter.increment(); //1
counter.increment(); //2
counter.increment(); //3
```

Notice that we always need to use the object reference followed by a dot and the name of the method.

Trying to do otherwise like destructuring the method will result in the function not being linked to the object anymore. Here is the same function invoked using the function form.

```
const increment = counter.increment;
increment();
//TypeError: Cannot read property 'count' of undefined
```

In this example, we are not calling **increment** as a method anymore, but as a function.

Invoking as Constructor

Before having classes JavaScript used function constructors to make building objects familiar to developers coming from a class-based language like Java.

Here is how it looks like to define a function and then invoked it as a constructor using the new operator.

```
function Counter(){
  this.count = 0;
}

Counter.prototype.increment = function(){
  this.count += 1;
  return this.count;
}

const counter = new Counter();
counter.increment(); //1
counter.increment(); //2
counter.increment(); //3
```

Function constructors are usually named starting with an uppercase letter. They are invoked using the new operator.

```
new Counter();
```

However, this syntax is now obsolete. We should use a class instead.

```
class Counter{
  constructor(){
    this.count = 0;
  }

  increment(){
    this.count += 1;
    return this.count;
  }
}

const counter = new Counter();
counter.increment(); //1
counter.increment(); //2
```

```
counter.increment(); //3
```

Invoking with call and apply

Functions are objects as such we can call methods on them.

The apply method invokes a function with a given this value and the arguments provided as an array.

Consider the previous sum function.

```
function sum(x, y){
   return x + y;
}
```

Here is the function invocation using the apply method. The this parameter is not used inside the function so we can use null as the first argument.

```
sum.apply(null, [1, 2]);
//3
```

The call method invokes a function with a given this value and the arguments provided separately.

```
sum.call(null, 1, 2);
//3
```

Now consider a function using the this parameter.

```
"use strict";

function increment(){
   this.count += 1;
   return this.count;
}
```

Invoking it like a function results in an error.

```
increment();
//TypeError: Cannot read property 'count' of undefined
```

Nevertheless, we can invoke it using the apply and call methods and provide the associated object referred to by the this parameter.

```
const counter = {
   count: 1
```

```
}
```

```
increment.call(counter); //2
increment.apply(counter); //3
```

Invoking a Recursive Function

A recursive function is a function that calls itself several times until a stop condition is met.

The `countDown` is a recursive function that calls itself as long as the input number is positive.

```
function countDown(number) {
   console.log(number);

   if (number > 0) {
     countDown(number - 1);
   }
}
```

```
countDown(3);
//3
//2
//1
//0
```

Function Objects

Functions are objects and like other objects, they can be sent to functions as arguments.

In the next example, the function `isEven` is sent as an argument to the `filter` array method.

```
function isEvent(n) {
   return n % 2 === 0;
}
```

```
const numbers = [1, 2, 3, 4];
const evenNumbers = numbers.filter(isEvent);
```

```
console.log(evenNumbers);
```

```
//[2, 4]
```

Objects can be returned from functions.

```
function getEmptyObject() {
  return {};
}
```

Functions like other objects can be also returned from functions.

```
function createFunction(x){
  return function(){};
}
```

Note that `function` is not the first keyword on the line, so we are returning a function expression.

Key Notes

- Functions can be created using function declarations, function expressions, and the arrow syntax.
- Functions can be called with any number of arguments. Extra arguments are ignored, missing parameters are set to `undefined`
- Functions can be invoked as functions, methods, constructors, and using the `call` and `apply` methods.
- Function expressions can be immediately invoked after creation.
- Functions are objects and as such can be sent as arguments to other functions or returned from functions.

Chapter 09: Function Declarations vs Arrow Functions

In this chapter, we will examine the most important differences between the arrow functions the standard function declarations.

Function Name

The arrow functions don't have a name but they may infer the name from the variable storing the function.

Here is an example of an arrow function stored in a variable. Checking the name property gives the variable name as a string.

```
const sum = (x, y) => x + y;

sum.name;
//'sum'

typeof sum.name;
//string
```

Functions created with the function declarations must have a name.

```
function sum(x, y){
  return x + y;
}

sum.name;
//'sum'
```

```
typeof sum.name;
//string
```

Function Hoisting

Functions declarations are hoisted to the top of their scope. That means we can use such a function before being declared. Below is an example.

```
max(1,2); //2

function max(x, y){
  return x > y ? x : y;
}
```

The arrow functions cannot be used before declaration.

```
max(1,2);
//Cannot access 'max' before initialization

const max = (x, y) => x > y ? x : y;
```

Self-Executing at Creation

The arrow syntax creates function expressions so they can be auto-invoked at creation. Here is an example.

```
(() => {
  console.log('app started');
})();
//'app started'
```

We cannot self-execute a function created with the function declaration. Once we try to do that it is no longer a function declaration but a function expression. In the next example, the `function` keyword is not the first on the line but the (character is. We have created a function expression.

```
(function(){
  console.log('app started');
})();
//'app started'
```

this

Arrow functions don't have their own `this` parameter which means they are a good fit for creating inner functions inside methods.

Consider the next example.

```
const message = {
  msg: 'Hi!',
  show(){
    const logMsg = () => {
      console.log(this.msg);
    }

    logMsg();
  }
}

message.show();
//'Hi!'
```

The `this` parameter from the `logMsg` inner function points to the same objects as the `this` parameter inside the `show` method.

Functions created with the function declaration have their own `this`. The following `logMsg` inner function does not refer to the same objects as the `this` parameter inside the `show` method.

```
const message = {
  msg: 'Hi!',
  show(){
    function logMsg(){
      console.log(this.msg);
    }

    logMsg();
  }
}

message.show();
//undefined
```

Function Method

Functions can be used as methods on objects. The this parameter establishes the connection between these functions and the associated object. It gives access to all the other properties on that object.

Because arrow functions don't have their own this pseudo argument we can't associate them with objects.

Here is what happens when trying to use an arrow function as a method.

```
"use strict";

const counter = {
  count: 0,
  increment: ()=> {
    this.count += 1;
    return this.count;
  },
  decrement: ()=> {
    this.count += 1;
    return this.count;
  }
}

counter.increment(); //NaN
counter.increment(); //NaN
counter.increment(); //NaN
```

The this parameter inside the increment and decrement functions point to the same object as the parent scope. The parent scope in our case is the global scope. The this parameter inside the arrow functions refers to the global object, not to the counter object.

Arrow functions should not be methods.

When using the function keyword in this context we are not dealing with function declarations but with function expressions. Nevertheless, because they have their own this parameter they can refer to the associated object.

```
const counter = {
  count: 0,
  increment: function(){
```

```
    this.count += 1;
    return this.count;
  },
  decrement: function(){
    this.count += 1;
    return this.count;
  }
}
```

```
counter.increment(); //1
counter.increment(); //2
counter.increment(); //3
```

The same methods can be written with the equivalent shorthand notation where the `function` keyword is no longer necessary.

```
const counter = {
  count: 0,
  increment(){
    this.count += 1;
    return this.count;
  },
  decrement(){
    this.count += 1;
    return this.count;
  }
}
```

Function Constructor

JavaScript tries to make the prototype system familiar to developers coming from a class-based language. Before having "classes" in the language, functions could be used as constructors to create objects.

```
function Todo(){}
const todo = new Todo();
//Todo {}
```

Arrow functions cannot be used as constructors. Doing so will result in an error being thrown.

```
const Todo = () => {}
const todo = new Todo();
```

```
//Todo is not a constructor
```

Key Notes

- The name is mandatory in function declarations. Arrow functions don't have a name but may infer one.
- Function declarations are hoisted to the top of their scope. Arrow functions are not hoisted.
- Function declarations cannot self-execute at creation. Arrow functions can auto-execute after the definition.
- Arrow functions don't have their own `this` and as such when defined inside methods the `this` parameter from the arrow functions refers to the same object as the one in the parent method.
- Arrow functions should not be methods or constructors.

Character 10: Arrays

An array is an indexed collection of values. A value in the array is called an element and has a numeric position called an index.

Arrays can be simply created with the array literal by wrapping several values separated by commas inside square brackets.

```
[1, 2, 3]
```

An empty array is one with no elements.

```
[]
```

Accessing Elements

We read an element at a given index using the square notation.

```
const letters = ['a', 'b', 'C'];

letters[0]
//'a'

letters[1]
//'b'
```

In a similar way, we can change the element at the specified index.

```
letters[2] = 'c';

console.log(letters);
//['a', 'b', 'c']
```

Arrays are Objects

JavaScript does not have "real" arrays. Arrays are in fact emulated using objects.

Let's consider the following array.

```
const greetings = [
  'Hello',
  'Good morning',
  'Good evening'
];
```

It is emulated using an object similar to the one below.

```
{
 '0' : 'Hello',
 '1' : 'Good morning',
 '2' : 'Good evening'
}
```

When we use numeric indexes we are in fact using string indexes. Rember that non-string keys are converted to strings, so numerical array indexes are converted to strings.

This is why we can access the same element using a numeric index but also with a string index.

```
greetings[1] === greetings['1']
//true
```

Even JavaScript tells us that an array is actually an object when using the `typeof` operator.

```
typeof greetings
//'object'
```

To check for an array we can use the `Array.isArray` utility.

```
Array.isArray(greetings)
//true
```

Length Property

Arrays have the `length` prop telling its "size".

```
const arr = ['A', 'B'];
```

```
console.log(arr.length)
//2
```

It is not really the size of the array but the last index plus 1.

```
const arr = [];
arr[5] = 'F';

console.log(arr.length)
//6
```

Adding and Removing

Arrays are dynamic collections without a fixed size. We can add, edit or delete elements on them.

The **push** method adds a new element to the end of the array.

The **pop** method removes the last element from the array.

The **push** and **pop** methods can be used to emulate a stack.

```
const stack = [];
stack.push('Red');      //["Red"]
stack.push('Yellow');   //["Red", "Yellow"]

const color = stack.pop();
console.log(color);
//"Yellow"

console.log(stack);
//["Red"]
```

A stack is a data structure storing a collection of elements, with two main operations:

- push, adding an element to the collection
- pop, removing the most recently added element that is still in the collection

The **shift** method removes the first element from an array.

```
const collors = ["Red", "Yellow", "Blue"];
```

```
const firstColor = collors.shift();
console.log(firstColor);
//"Red"

console.log(collors);
// ["Yellow", "Blue"]
```

The shift and push methods can be used to create a queue.

A queue is a data structure storing a collection of elements, with two main operations:

- enqueue, adding an element to the end of the collection. This is the task of the push array method.
- dequeue, removing an element from the front of the collection. This is done with the shift array method.

The better way to work with arrays is to use the array methods, not with loops.

Reversing Order

The reverse method reverses the order of the elements in an array.

```
const letters = ['A', 'B', 'C']

letters.reverse();
//["C", "B", "A"]
```


Sorting

The sort method converts elements to strings and sorts them alphabetically. This, of course, works great for sorting strings.

```
const fruits = ["Lemon", "Apple", "Mango"];
fruits.sort()

console.log(fruits);
//["Apple", "Lemon", "Mango"]
```

Remember that the sort changes the input array.

Sorting Arrays of Numbers

As said `sort` converts values to strings before sorting them. This serves us well for sorting strings but does not work for numbers. Check the following example.

```
const numbers = [-1, -3, -2];
console.log(numbers.sort());
//[-1, -2, -3]
```

When numbers are sorted as strings, `'-2'` comes after `'-1'`.

However, we can fix this by providing a compare function.

```
function asc(a, b){
  if(a < b) return -1;
  if(a > b) return 1;
  return 0;
}
```

```
const numbers = [-1, -3, -2];
console.log(numbers.sort(asc));
//[-3, -2, -1]
```

The compare function defines the sort order. It takes two elements `a` and `b` and returns `-1` if `a` comes before `b`, `1` if `a` comes after `b`, and `0` if the order remains unchanged.

`asc` is the compare function.

Here is a short version of the previous compare function that can be used to sort numbers ascending.

```
function asc(a, b){
  return a - b;
}
```

Searching

The array has methods for searching primitive values: `indexOf`, `lastIndexOf`, and `includes`.

`indexOf` gets the first index of a given element. It returns `-1` if the element is not found.

`lastIndexOf()` returns the last index of a given element. It returns `-1` if the element is not found.

`includes` checks if a given element exists and returns `true` or `false` as appropriate.

```
const letters = ['A', 'B', 'C'];

letters.indexOf('A')
//0

letters.lastIndexOf('A')
//0

letters.includes('B')
//true
```

On the other hand, searching in an array of objects is done with `find`, `findIndex`, `filter`, `some` and `every`.

filter

The `filter` method returns an array with all elements that pass the test from a predicate function.

A predicate is a function that takes an element returns a boolean.

The `Boolean` built-in utility can convert any value into a boolean. It is a predicate function.

Below is an example of removing all falsy values from an array and keeping only the truthy values.

```
const arr = [1, 2, undefined, null, NaN, 0, 3];

const newArr = arr.filter(Boolean);
//[1, 2, 3]
```

Now let's search values in an array of objects. Consider the next array.

```
const characters = [
  { value: 'A', type: 'letter'},
  { value: 'B', type: 'letter'},
  { value: '1', type: 'number'}
];
```

In order to find all characters that are letters, we can provide the following predicate function.

```
function isLetter(char){
  return char.type === "letter";
}
```

The `filter` method can then be used to return all letter character objects from the array.

```
const letters = characters.filter(isLetter);
//[
//{value: "A", type: "letter"}
//{value: "B", type: "letter"}
//]
```

find

The `find` method returns the first element in an array that pass the test from a predicate function.

```
const firstLetter = characters.find(isLetter);
//{value: "A", type: "letter"}
```

The `find` method stops after finding the first element. The `filter` method does not stop. It applies the predicate function to all elements.

findIndex

The `findIndex` method returns the index of the first element in an array that passes the test from a predicate function.

```
const firstLetterIndex = characters.findIndex(isLetter);
//0
```

some

The `some` method checks if at least one element in an array pass the test from a predicate function.

```
const hasLetters = characters.some(isLetter);
//true
```

every

The `every` method checks if all the elements in an array pass the test from a predicate function.

```
const allLetters = characters.every(isLetter);
console.log(allLetters)
//false
```

Transforming

The `map` method transforms an array into a new array using a mapping function. It calls the given mapping function once for each element in an array.

Consider the following array containing both numbers and string representation of numbers.

```
const arr = ['1', '2', 3, '6'];
```

The `Number` built-in utility can convert any value into a number. We can use it as the mapping function to convert the previous array into an array of numbers.

```
const numbers = arr.map(Number);
//[1, 2, 3, 6]
```

Reducing

The `reduce` method aggregates the array to a single value using a reducer function.

The reducer function takes the accumulator, the current element, the current index, and returns the new accumulator.

Consider the `max` reducer function returning the maximum of two numbers. It takes the current accumulator, meaning the current maximum value. If the accumulator is greater than the current number it returns the accumulator otherwise it returns the current value.

```
function max(acc, value){
   return acc > value ? acc : value;
}
```

We can now use the `max` reducer to compute the maxim number in an array of numbers.

```
const arr = [1, 5, 3, 2];

arr.reduce(max)
//5
```

The reducer function is called for each element in the array.

```
initial acc = 1
acc = 1, element = 5 -> acc = 5
acc = 5, element = 3 -> acc = 5
acc = 5, element = 2 -> acc = 5
```

reduce can be called with and without an initial value. When called with an initial value it starts from the first element. When called without an initial value it considers the first element as the initial value and starts from the second element.

reduceRight works in a similar way but starts from the end of the array.

forEach

forEach calls a function for each element in the array. It takes as parameters both the current value and the current index.

```
const chars = ['A', 'B', undefined, 'C'];

function log(value, index){
  console.log(`${index}: ${value}`);
}

chars.forEach(log);
//"0: A"
//"1: B"
//"2: undefined"
//"3: C"
```

forEach does not stop. every/some can be used to iterate and stop based on the returned value.

The following processing loop stops at the first falsy value.

```
const chars = ['A', 'B', undefined, 'C'];

function log(value, index){
```

```
    console.log(`${index}: ${value}`);
    return Boolean(value);
}

chars.every(log);
//"0: A"
//"1: B"
//"2: undefined"
```

concat

The concat method returns a new array with all the elements from the current array and other arrays provided as input.

```
const letters = ['A', 'B'];
const numbers = ['1', '2'];
const chars = letters.concat(numbers);
console.log(chars);
//["A", "B", "1", "2"]
```

slice

The slice(start, end) method selects the elements from the array starting at the given start index, and ending at, but not including the given end index.

```
const letters = ['A', 'B', 'C', 'D', 'E'];
const part = letters.slice(1, 3);
console.log(part);
// ["B", "C"]
```

Both the start and the end indexes are optional. If they are omitted a shallow copy of the array is created.

```
const clone = letters.slice();
//["A", "B", "C", "D", "E"]

clone === letters
//false
```

If the end index is omitted all the elements till the end of the array are selected.

```
const part = letters.slice(1);
```

```
//["B", "C", "D", "E"]
```

Initialization

There are cases when we want to create an array filled with default values. For small arrays, of course, we can just write down the values when declaring the array but for larger arrays, a nicer system may be needed.

```
const arr = [false, false, false, false, false];
```

Initialization with Primitives

The `Array` built-in function can be used to create an array with the specified length but with no actual values in it.

`Array(5)` gives an array of length 5 but with no values.

```
const arr = Array(5);
console.log(arr.length);
//5
```

The `fill(value, start, end)` method changes all elements in an array to a default value. It begins from the start index (default 0) to the end index (default `array.length`) and returns the modified array. Both `start` and `end` indexes are options. `fill` is an impure method, it changes the input array.

Below is an example of resetting all values of an array to `false`.

```
const arr = [undefined, undefined, undefined];
arr.fill(false);

console.log(arr);
//[false, false, false]
```

Let's get back to our case and use both the `Array` built-in function and the `fill` method to declare and initialized all values of an array with `false`.

```
const arr = Array(5).fill(false);
//[false, false, false, false, false]
```

Initialization with Objects

`fill` works well with primitive values, but when called with a default object it reuses the same object for all elements.

```
const arr = Array(5).fill({});
arr[0].msg = 'Hi';

console.log(arr);
//[
//{msg: "Hi"},
//{msg: "Hi"},
//{msg: "Hi"},
//{msg: "Hi"},
//{msg: "Hi"},
//]
```

We need to find a way to set each element to a different object.

We can use the previous approach and create an array initialized with `undefined` values.

```
const arr = Array(5).fill();
//[undefined, undefined, undefined, undefined, undefined]
```

Then on this kind of array, we can map each element to a new empty object.

The `map` method creates a new array filled with the results of calling a mapping function on each element in the array.

```
const arr = Array(5).fill().map(()=>({}));
arr[0].msg = 'Hi';

console.log(arr);
//[
//0: {msg: "Hi"}
//1: {}
//2: {}
//3: {}
//4: {}
//]
```

Our mapping function `()=>({})` just creates a new empty object.

Spread Operator

Spread syntax (. . .) allows an iterable object like an array to be expanded in cases where several arguments or elements are expected.

We can use the spread operator to spread all values from the array into a new array and create a shallow clone using the array literal syntax.

```
const arr = [1, 2, 3];
const clone = [...arr];
//[1, 2, 3]
```

An alternative for creating an array filled with undefined is to use the spread operator. Below is an example.

```
const arr = [...Array(5)];
//[undefined, undefined, undefined, undefined, undefined]
```

The Math.max function for example accepts several arguments and returns the maximum value.

```
Math.max(1, 2, 3);
//3
```

We can use the spread operator to expand the array into the arguments expected by the Math.max utility.

```
const arr = [1, 2, 3];
Math.max(...arr)
//3
```

Converting to a String

We transform an array of elements into a single string using the join method.

The join array method creates a new string by concatenating all of the elements in an array using a specified string separator string.

Here is an example.

```
const arr = ['Fire', 'and', 'Blood'];
const text = arr.join(' ');
//'Fire and Blood'
```

If no separator is provided a comma is used as default.

```
const arr = ['Fire', 'and', 'Blood'];
const csv = arr.join();
//'Fire,and,Blood'
```

When the array has just one item, it will be converted into a string without any separator.

```
const arr = ['Winterfell'];
arr.join('-');
//'Winterfell'
```

Key Notes

- The array literal is the simplest way to create an array
- `Array.isArray` can detect an array.
- `push` and `pop` add and remove an element to/from the end of an array.
- `filter` selects elements from the array based on the test provided by a predicate function.
- `map` transforms an array into a new array by mapping each element using a mapping function.
- `reduce` aggregates all the elements from the array into a single value using a reducer function.
- `sort` sorts an array using a compare function.
- `reduce` can start from both the start and the end of the array. `map` and `filter` can start only from the beginning.
- `join` concatenates all of the elements from the array into a string using a separator.
- `Array(length)` creates an array with the specified length but with no values.
- `fill` populates elements from the array with the specified value.

Chapter 11: Strings vs Arrays of Characters

In a sense, we can think of a string as an immutable array of characters.

We can actually create a string from an array using the `join('')` method, and an array of characters from a string using the `Array.from` utility.

```
const text = "ABC";

const arr = Array.from(text);
//['A', 'B', 'C']

arr.join('') === text
//true
```

Length Property

Both strings and arrays have the `length` property.

The `length` property does no return the number of characters in a string as expected but the number of UTF-16 code units. For strings containing characters that need two UTF-16 code units the `length` returns the wrong size.

```
const text = 'AB☺';
word.length
//4
```

The `length` of an array of characters returns the correct number of characters.

```
['A', 'B', '☺'].length
```

//3

Accessing Elements

Both strings and arrays allow retrieving an element at a specific index using the bracket notation. Consider the next example.

```
const text = "ABC";
cont char = text[0];
//'A'
```

Both strings and arrays use zero-based indexing. The first character stays at position 0.

Remember that the bracket notation on strings delivers a new string of length 1 containing a character. The bracket notation is used only to retrieve a new string containing a character not to change it.

The following code trying to change a character at a specific index does not work. Strings are immutable.

```
const text = "ABC";
text[0] = "D";
//Cannot assign to read only property '0' of string 'ABC'
```

This is is different from the array where the bracket notation allows to change the value at the specified index.

```
const arr = ['A', 'B', 'C'];
arr[0] = 'D';
//["D", "B", "C"]
```

Retrieving an element from the array returns the value at that index, not its copy.

Accessing a character using an index on a string does not give the correct result when the character takes two code units.

```
const text = '☺A'
console.log(text[0]); //�
console.log(text[1]); //�
```

Accessing a character by index in an array of characters returns the correct result.

```
const arr = ['☺', 'A'];
```

```
console.log(arr[0]); //'☺'
console.log(arr[1]); //'A'
```

Equality

Two strings containing the same characters are equal. That is not the same for arrays. Two arrays containing the same values are not equal.

```
"ABC" === "ABC"
//true
```

```
['A', 'B', 'C'] === ['A', 'B', 'C']
//false
```

The `indexOf`, `slice` and `concat` methods can be used for both strings and arrays.

indexOf

The `indexOf` method returns the index of the first occurrence of a specified text in a string. When the text is not found it returns `-1`.

On strings `indexOf` can search for more than one character. In an array of characters, we can search only for one element, meaning a single character.

```
const text = "Fly High";
const firstIndex = text.indexOf("High");
//4
```

```
const arr = ['F', 'l', 'y', ' ', 'H', 'i', 'g', 'h'];
const firstIndex = arr.indexOf('l');
//1
```

slice

The `slice(start, end)` method returns the part of a string between the `start` and `end` indexes.

The `slice(start, end)` method on an array returns a shallow copy of a portion of it into a new array.

Applying the same `slice` method of both strigs and arrays gives a similar result.

```
const text = 'ABCDE';
const arr = ['A', 'B', 'C', 'D', 'E'];

console.log(text.slice(1, 3));
//'BC'

arr.slice(1, 3);
//['B', 'C']
```

concat

The concat method concatenates all the string arguments to the original string and returns a new string.

```
"A".concat("BC")
//"ABC"

"A".concat("BC", "DE");
//"ABCDE"
```

The concat method on an array creates a new array containing the current elements followed by the elements of the given arrays arguments.

```
['A'].concat(['B', 'C'])
//['A', 'B', 'C']

['A'].concat(['B', 'C'], ['D', 'E'])
//['A', 'B', 'C', 'D', 'E' ]
```

The concat method works in a similar way on both strings and arrays.

Iterable

Strings are iterable. We can use the for/of loop on them.

```
for (const char of "ABC") {
  console.log(char);
}
//'A'
//'B'
//'C'
```

It also works correctly when dealing with characters taking more code units.

```
for (const char of "A☺") {
  console.log(char);
}
//'A'
//'☺'
```

Note that loops using an index do not give the correct result when dealing with characters taking two code units. It returns two different unknown characters in our example using the emoji character.

```
const text = "A☺";
for (let i = 0; i < text.length; i++){
  console.log(text[i])
}
//A
//�
//�
```

Both for/of and for loops work correctly on an array of characters.

```
const arr = ['A', '☺'];

for (const char of arr) {
  console.log(char);
}
//'A'
//'☺'

for (let i = 0; i < arr.length; i++){
  console.log(arr[i])
}
//'A'
//'☺'
```

Array Destructuring

The destructuring assignment syntax makes it possible to unpack values from arrays into distinct variables.

Below is an example of extracting the first two values from an array into two variables.

```
const [first, second] = ['A', 'B', 'C'];
console.log(first); //'A'
```

```
console.log(second); //'B'
```

In a similar way, we can use the array destructuring syntax to extract letters from a string. Consider the next code.

```
const [first, second] = "ABC";
console.log(first); //'A'
console.log(second); //'B'
```

It is important to note that the destructuring syntax gives the correct letters even when the character takes two code units.

```
const [first, second] = '☺Hi!'
console.log(first); //'☺'
console.log(second); //'H'
```

Key Notes

- Both strings and arrays have index access and the `length` property.
- The `indexOf`, `slice`, and the `contact` methods are available on both strings and arrays.
- Strings are immutable. None of the string methods change the original string.
- Strings are array-like. They can be converted to an array of characters using the `Array.from` utility.
- Arrays of characters can be transformed into strings using the `join('')` method.

Chapter 12: Dates

Date objects represent dates and times and are created using the `Date` constructor.

Current Date

A date object expressing the current date and time can be built using the `Date` constructor with no arguments.

```
const currentDate = new Date();

console.log(currentDate);
//Mon Jan 03 2022 10:15:30 GMT+0100 (CET)
```

Custom Date

A date object representing a specific date and time can be created by sending up to seven arguments to the `Date` constructor.

```
new Date(year, month, day, hours, minutes, seconds, msec)
```

Below is an example:

```
const date = new Date(2021, 0, 1, 10, 0);
//Fri Jan 01 2021 10:00:00 GMT+0100 (CET)
```

Pay attention to the inconsistency between month and day. The second argument, the month, starts from 0. 0 represents January, 1 means February, and so on. The third argument, the day, starts from 1.

Not all arguments are mandatory. In fact, we can create a new date object using just the year and the month.

```
const date = new Date(2021, 0);
//Fri Jan 01 2021 00:00:00 GMT+0100 (CET)
```

Methods

The date object has several methods for extracting or changing parts of the date object.

The getFullYear method returns the full year of a date, in 4 digits.

The getMonth method gives the month (0 to 11).

The getDate method returns the day of the month (1 to 31).

The getHours method returns the hour (0 to 23).

The getMinutes method returns the minutes (0 to 59).

The getSeconds method returns the seconds (0 to 59).

Below is an example using all the previous methods to extract parts of a date object.

```
const date = new Date(2022, 0, 1, 10, 15, 30);

date.getFullYear(); //2022
date.getMonth();    //0
date.getDate();     //1
date.getHours();    //10
date.getMinutes();  //15
date.getSeconds();  //30
```

All the previous methods have associated set methods: setFullYear, setMonth, setDate, setHours, setMinutes, and setSeconds.

The toDateString method returns the date part of a date object as a string. The returned string does not contain the time.

The toTimeString method returns the time part of a date object as a string.

```
const date = new Date(2022, 0, 1, 10, 15, 30);

date.toDateString();
//Sat Jan 01 2022

date.toTimeString();
//10:15:30 GMT+0200 (Eastern European Standard Time)
```

ISO String Format

The `Date` constructor correctly converts ISO 8601 dates strings into date objects.

The ISO 8601 is an international standard for representing dates and times. `YYYY-MM-DD` is an example of ISO 8601 syntax for defining only the date part. For instance, `2021-01-15` is the representation of the 15th of January 2021. The `Date` constructor can parse such a string and build a date object.

```
const date = new Date('2021-01-15');

date.toDateString();
//Fri Jan 15 2021
```

The `YYYY-MM-DDTHH:MM:SSZ` syntax defines a date including a time part with hours, minutes, and seconds. The date and time are separated with a capital T. The UTC time is defined with the capital letter Z.

```
const date = new Date("2021-01-15T10:10:00Z");

date.toDateString();
//Fri Jan 15 2021

date.toTimeString();
//12:10:00 GMT+0200 (Eastern European Standard Time)
```

The `toISOString` method returns the string representation of the date in the ISO format.

```
const date = new Date("2021-01-15T10:10:00Z");

date.toISOString();
//2021-01-15T10:10:00.000Z
```

Numeric Representation

Dates have also a numeric representation called the timestamp. It represents the number of milliseconds since 1st of January, 1970, in the UTC time.

The `Date.now` utility returns the current time as a timestamp.

```
const timestamp = Date.now();
```

```
//1641196129722
```

Invoking the `Date` constructor with a single argument, `new Date(msec)` builds a new date object by adding the number of milliseconds to January 01, 1970, according to UTC time.

Knowing that 1 hour has `3_600_000` milliseconds next we create a date object and then get back the number of milliseconds.

```
const date = new Date(3_600_000);

date.getTime();
//3600000
```

The `getTime` method returns the number of milliseconds since 1st of January, 1970.

Notice that when the `Date` constructor is called with one argument, the first and only argument represents the number of milliseconds. When it is invoked with at least two arguments, the first one represents the year.

We can convert the date to the timestamp representation using the `Number` built-in function or with the `getTime` and `valueOf` methods.

The `valueOf` method returns the primitive representation of an object.

```
const now = new Date();

now.getTime() === now.valueOf();
//true

Number(now) === now.valueOf();
//true
```

UTC vs Local Time

UTC stands for Universal Time Coordinated. Prior to being adopted as the official abbreviation, this time was called Greenwich Mean Time (GMT) and it is also known as "Z time". This is where the capital letter `Z` in the ISO format comes from.

In order to get the local time, we need to subtract a certain number of hours from UTC depending on the timezone of the local time.

For example, the Central European Time (CET) is 1 hour ahead of the

UTC time. It means that when the UTC time is Fri Jan 01, 2021, 10:10, the local CET time is Fri Jan 01, 2021, 11:10.

The `getTimezoneOffset` method of a date object returns this timezone offset. It returns the difference in minutes. If the returned value is positive, the local timezone is behind the UTC and if it is negative, the local timezone is ahead of UTC. The returned value is not constant as it depends on daylight saving. For example, during summer the CET time changes to Central European Summer Time (CEST) which is 2 hours ahead of the UTC time.

The next example shows a negative timezone offset. The local time is 2 hours ahead of the UTC time.

```
const offset = new Date().getTimezoneOffset();
//-120
```

The time-zone offset is the difference, in minutes, between UTC and local time. The local time depends on the timezone of the browser or the operating system where the browser runs. The timezone offset can only be read, it cannot be changed from the JavaScript language.

The JavaScript date object is stored as UTC, and most of the methods missing the UTC abbreviation from their name usually work with the date in local time.

There are a few exceptions. The `getTime` return the number of milliseconds since 1970, according to the UTC time. The `toISOString` returns the date in UTC time. In this case, it can be easily noticed because the date string ends in the letter `Z`.

All the date methods for extracting parts of the date discussed so far have UTC equivalents. Remember that `getFullYear`, `getMonth`, `getDate`, `getHours`, `getMinutes`, `getSeconds` return the local time. Their UTC equivalents `getUTCFullYear`, `getUTCMonth`, `getUTCDate`, `getUTCHours`, `getUTCMinutes`, `getUTCSeconds` return the UTC time.

Next, we are going to check what kind of dates are created when passing different arguments to the `Date` constructor.

Invocation with Several Arguments

When calling the `Date` constructor with more than two arguments we are passing the local time. Check the next example where the local time is 2 hours ahead of the UTC time.

```
const date = new Date(2021, 0, 15, 10, 10);

date.getTimezoneOffset();
//-120

date.getUTCHours(); //8
date.getHours();    //10
```

As you noticed, the hour mentioned in the Date constructor is a local hour. In fact, all the arguments passed to the Date constructor this way refer to the local time.

Invocation with Milliseconds

When calling the Date constructor with one argument it adds the number of milliseconds to January 1, 1970, 00:00:00 in the UTC time.

Check the next example adding 1 hour in milliseconds (3_600_000). In this case, where the local time is 2 hours ahead of the UTC time, the local hour is 3.

```
const date = new Date(3_600_000);

date.getTimezoneOffset();
//-120

date.getUTCHours(); //1
date.getHours();    //3
```

Invocation Using Date.UTC

Let's get back to our previous example.

```
const date = new Date(2021, 0, 15, 10, 10);

date.toUTCString();
//Fri, 15 Jan 2021 08:10:00 GMT
```

The toUTCString method returns a string representing the date in the UTC time zone.

What if we want to build a date object where the UTC time is 10:10.

The `Date.UTC` utility accepts several arguments similar to the `Date` constructor and returns the number of milliseconds since January 1, 1970, 00:00:00 UTC.

We can create a date object using arguments that refer to the UTC time by passing the result of the `Date.UTC` utility to the `Date` constuctor.

```
const date = new Date(Date.UTC(2021, 0, 15, 10, 10));

date.getTimezoneOffset();
//-120

date.getUTCHours(); //10
date.getHours();     //12
```

Notice that in this case, the hour specified in the constructor is the UTC hour. In fact, all the arguments from the `new Date(Date.UTC())` constructor, refer to the UTC time.

Invoking with an ISO String

When invoking the `Date` constructor with an ISO formatted date string the string itself specifies a local or a UTC time.

When the capital Z letter is at the end of the string we are dealing with a UTC date.

```
const date = new Date('2021-01-15T10:10:00.000Z');

date.getTimezoneOffset();
//-120

date.getUTCHours(); //10
date.getHours();     //12
```

When the capital Z letter is missing at the end of the date string including the time we are dealing with a local date.

```
const date = new Date('2021-01-15T10:10:00.000');

date.getUTCHours(); //8
date.getHours();     //10
```

Key Notes

A date object representing the current date and time is built by invoking the `Date` constructor with no argument. The invoking creates a local date.

A specific date object can be created by calling the `Date` constructor with more than two arguments, representing the year, month, day, hours, minutes, seconds, and milliseconds. This invoking creates a local date.

Date objects and can be built from an ISO string representation. The provided ISO string value defines a local or UTC date.

Invoking the `Date` constructor with only one argument expects the number of milliseconds since 1 January 1970, in UTC time. This invocation applies the number of milliseconds to a UTC time.

While the value stored behind the date object is in UTC format most of the methods missing the UTC abbreviation from their name work with local date and time, which means they take into consideration the timezone offset.

Chapter 13: Regular Expressions

Regular expressions are patterns used for matching characters on strings. For example, they can be used to search for a text in a string, replace a part of a text, or extract information from a string.

Creation

Regular expressions can be built using a regular expression literal or the `RegExp` constructor.

Below is an example of a regular expression literal. Notice that the pattern is defined between slashes (/). It matches a digit from 0 to 9 in a text.

```
/[0-9]/
```

Below is the same regular expression created with the `RegExp` constructor.

```
new RegExp('[0-9]')
```

Literal vs Constructor

The regular expression built with a literal is created when the script is loaded and cannot be changed. The regular expression defined with the `RegExp` constructor is created at runtime and can be modified. When we want to create a regular expression based on a string, being that user input, for example, we need to use the constructor.

Next is such an example of a regular expression that matches strings starting with a specific user input text.

```
const userInputText = "ab";
const startsWithRegExp = new RegExp(`^${userInputText}`);
```

```
startsWithRegExp.test("ab1"); //true
startsWithRegExp.test("bc1"); //false
```

Methods

In JavaScript, regular expressions are objects so they have methods. These
are `exec` and `test`.

The `test` method takes a string and verifies if the string matches the
regular expression pattern. It returns a boolean.

Here is how we can check if a text contains only numbers.

```
const onlyNumbersRegex = /^[0-9]+$/;
const hasOnlyNumbers = onlyNumbersRegex.test("12345");
//true
```

Below is a text that does not pass the regular expression pattern. It
should have only numbers and it includes also a letter.

```
onlyNumbersRegex.test("12345A");
//false
```

The `exec` method makes a search for a match in a given string. It returns
an array, or `null` when no match is found.

Check the next example where the `exec` method returns the first match
of a number in the given text.

```
const onlyNumbersRegex = /[0-9]+/;
const result = onlyNumbersRegex.exec("123 234");
//['123']
```

In the returned array the first element (`'123'`) represents the first match.

Special Characters

A simple regular expression like `/abc/` matches exactly that, the text
`"abc"`. Regular expressions include special characters that allow defining
patterns.

For example, `\w` matches any alphanumeric character including the underscore. That means it matches the letter characters (`a-z`, `A-Z`), the Arabic
numbers (`0-9`), and also the underscore (`_`) character.

`\s` matches any white-space character.

Here is an example of a regular expression matching alphanumerics followed by a single space.

```
const regExp = /\w+\s/;
```

The + symbol matches one or more characters. `\w+` means that at least one alphanumeric character is expected. `\s` indicates that one space is expected after that.

In strings, the backslash character (\) is used to escape single or double-quotes. The backslash character itself has to be escaped in strings (`'\\'`). In regular expressions defined with the `RegExp` constructor the backslash character (\) needs to be escaped.

```
const regExp = new RegExp('\\w+\\s');
```

Here are a few other important special characters in regular expressions:

- ^ matches the beginning of the text
- $ matches the end of a text
- `\p{L}` matches any Unicode letter
- `\d` matches all digits from zero to nine
- `[abc]` matches any one of the enclosed characters. A range of characters can be specified by using a hyphen/minus character (-).

Consider the following regular expressions for a better understanding of the special characters.

The `^ab` pattern matches a text starting with `ab` letters.

The `ab$` pattern matches a text ending with `ab` letters.

The `^\d+$` pattern matches a text containing only digits.

The `^[124]+$` pattern matches a text containing only the digits 1, 2 and 4.

The `^[0-3]+$` pattern matches a text containing only digits from 0 to 3.

Flags

Regular expressions allow optional flags for enabling features like global searching or enabling various Unicode-related features.

- g stays for global search

- i enables a case-insensitive search
- u enables Unicode-related features

Here is how a flag can be used in regular expression literals:

```
const regExp = /pattern/flags;
```

Flags can be sent as the second argument for the RegExp constructor.

```
const regExp = new RegExp('pattern', 'flags');
```

For example, consider that we want to create a pattern matching a name containing any kind of letter. The following pattern using the \w special character fails to match a name containing the letter é.

```
const pattern = /^\w+$/
pattern.test("Asterix"); //true
pattern.test("Astérix"); //false
```

\w matches both letters, numbers, and the underscore character. We can improve the previous pattern and match only letters by defining the exact letters we are looking for.

```
const pattern = /^[a-zA-Zé]+$/
pattern.test("Asterix"); //true
pattern.test("Astérix"); //true
```

That may work for our special case but the earlier pattern does not match any letter for any language. The \p{L} symbol denotes a letter in any language, but in order to use it, the regular expression must have the Unicode flag.

```
const pattern = /^\p{L}+$/u
pattern.test("Asterix"); //true
pattern.test("Astérix"); //true
```

String Methods

A few string methods can get regular expressions as arguments. These methods are: match, matchAll, replace, search and split.

match

The match method takes a regular expression and returns an array with all of the matches, or null if no match is found.

```
const numbersRegExp = new RegExp('[0-9]+');
const text = 'ABC123ABC567';

const matches = text.match(numbersRegExp);
//['123']
```

We haven't used the global flag (g) when creating the regular expression, so it returns an array containing only the first match. To get an array with all the numbers found in the text we need the global flag.

```
const numbersRegExp = new RegExp('[0-9]+', 'g');
const text = 'ABC123ABC567';

const matches = text.match(numbersRegExp);
//['123', '567']
```

matchAll

The `matchAll` method takes a regular expression and returns an iterator of all matching results. The input expression pattern needs the global flag.

```
const numbersRegExp = new RegExp('[0-9]+', 'g');
const text = 'ABC123ABC567';
const matches = text.matchAll(numbersRegExp);

for(match of matches){
  console.log(match)
}
//['123', index: 3]
//['567', index: 9]
```

replace

The `replace` method can take a pattern and a `replacement` text and returns a new string with one or all matches of a `pattern` replaced by the `replacement` text. If the regular expression `pattern` does not contain the global flag only the first occurrence is replaced.

The next example shows how to replace the first digit in the string with 0.

```
const regExp = new RegExp('[0-9]');
const text = 'The acount number is 12345';
```

```
const formattedText = text.replace(regExp, '0');
//The acount number is 02345
```

All occurrences of the given pattern are replaced when the global flag is used.

```
const regExp = new RegExp('[0-9]', 'g');
const text = 'The acount number is 12345';

const formattedText = text.replace(regExp, '0');
//The acount number is 00000
```

search

The `search` method takes a pattern and returns the index position of the first matched text.

The next example detects the position of the first number in the text.

```
const numbersRegExp = new RegExp('[0-9]+');
const text = 'ABC123ABC567';

text.search(numbersRegExp);
//3
```

split

The `split` accepts a regular expression separator pattern and returns a new list of substrings. The division in substrings is done by searching for the given pattern.

The next regular expression matches any combination of comma (,), dot (\.), question mark (\?) and space (\s) characters.

```
const separatorsRegx = /[,\.\?\s]+/
```

Next, the `split` method divides the given text into words using the separator pattern.

```
const text = "Quanta fretta, ma dove corri, dove vai?"
const words = text.split(separatorsRegx);
//['Quanta', 'fretta', 'ma', 'dove', 'corri',
// 'dove', 'vai', '']
```

Key Notes

Regular expressions are mainly used for text processing.

The `test` method on the regular expression object verifies if a given text respects a pattern.

To extract out matching strings from a given text the `match` method on strings can be used.

The `replace` method on strings allows replacing the first or all the matches.

The index position of the first match can be found using the `search` method on a string.

The `split` method can divide a string into a list of substrings by searching for a pattern.

Chapter 14: Primitives vs Objects

This chapter looks at the main differences between primitives and objects.

Almost Everything is an Object

In JavaScript, an object is just a collection of key-value pairs.

Functions

Are functions also objects?

Let's try to create a function and start adding properties to it:

```
const movie = function(){};
movie.title = 'Toc Toc'; //prop added
movie.year = 2017; //prop added
delete movie.year; //prop deleted
```

Consider the following `Integer` function that converts other values to integers:

```
const Integer = function(value){
  return parseInt(value);
};

Integer('123');
//123
```

We can add to it the `isInteger` property storing a function.

```
Integer.isInteger = function(value){
  return value === Number.parseInt(value);
```

```
}
```

We are then able to call the `isInteger` utility.

```
Integer.isInterger(123);
//true
```

At this point, we can say that a function is a callable object.

```
const x = function(){ return 'Hi' };
x.type = 'Greeting';

x();

x.type
//'Greeting'
```

Primitives

Are primitives objects? Can we add properties to them?

Consider the next example:

```
const text = "Hi";
text.type = 'greeting';

console.log(text.type);
//undefined
```

We cannot add, edit, or delete properties on primitives like strings, but we can access methods on them as if they were objects.

```
'in bruges'.toUpperCase();
// "IN BRUGES"
```

When trying to access the `toUpperCase` property on a string, JavaScript builds a temporary wrapper object around it and accesses the `toUpperCase` property. After the property is accessed, the wrapper object is eligible to be destroyed.

null and undefined

`null` and `undefined` are still primitives, but they are not treated as objects.

null and `undefined` are not converted to object wrappers. Trying to access properties on those primitives will throw an error.

```
null.msg;
// Uncaught TypeError: Cannot read property 'msg' of null

undefined.length;
// Uncaught TypeError: Cannot read property 'msg' of undefined
```

Of course, we cannot add properties to these two values.

```
const x = null;

x.msg = 'Hi';
//Uncaught TypeError: Cannot set property 'msg' of null
```

Nonetheless, JavaScript is misleading and says that `null` is an object:

```
typeof(null);
//'object'
```

Primitive Wrapper Objects

Except for `null` and `undefined`, all primitive values have a related function object with several uses. These are:

- `String` for the string primitive
- `Number` for the number primitive
- `BigInt` for the bigint primitive
- `Boolean` for the boolean primitive
- `Symbol` for the symbol primitive

Converting to Primitives

The `Number`, `BigInt`, `Boolean`, and `String` can be used to convert any value to specific types. `Number` converts values to numbers, `Boolean` to booleans, `String` to strings and so on.

```
Number('1')
//1

String(1)
//'1'
```

```
Boolean(0)
//false
```

Storing Utility Functions

Besides that, they are used for holding utility functions acting like an object.

The `Number` function for example is also an object and holds utility methods like `isInteger`, `isNaN`, etc. It contains data properties like `Number.EPSILON` or `Number.MAX_VALUE`. The `Symbol` function object holds the `Symbol.for` and `Symbol.keyFor` utilities.

Creating Wrapper Objects

When a method is called on a primitive, JavaScript converts it into an object using the `Number` , `BigInt`, `String`, `Boolean`, `Symbol` wrapper functions.

Here is an example of how the `Number` constructor can be used to build a wrapper object.

```
const no = 1;
typeof no
//'number'

const noObj = new Number(1);
typeof noObj
//'object'
```

Then JavaScript uses the newly created object to call methods. The wrapper's `valueOf()` method returns the primitive value.

```
noObj.valueOf() === no
//true
```

Storing the prototypes

All numbers inherit methods from the `Number.prototype` object. Big integers inherit properties from `BigInt.prototype`, strings from `String.prototype` , and booleans from `Boolean.prototype`.

Reference vs Value Types

When assigning a primitive to a variable for example the whole value is copied.

```
const a = 1;
const b = a;
```

When assigning an object to a variable only the reference to it is copied. In the next example, both variables point to the same object.

```
const a = { value: 1};
const b = a;

a.value = 2;
console.log(b.value)
//2
```

The difference can be better seen when invoking a function. Here is the changeTo function called with primitive values.

```
function changeTo(value, newValue){
   value = newValue;
}

const a = 1;
changeTo(a, 2);

console.log(a);
//1
```

Below is a similar changeTo function but this time the first argument is an object. The input object is modified inside the function. Both the a variable and the obj parameter hold the same reference. They point to the same object.

```
function changeTo(obj, newValue){
   obj.value = newValue;
}

const a = {value : 1};
changeTo(a, 2);

console.log(a);
```

```
//{value: 2}
```

Primitives are compared by value, objects by reference.

```
1 === 1
//true
```

```
'Hi' === 'Hi'
//true
```

```
true === true
//true
```

```
[] === []
//false
```

Two different objects are not equal even if they have properties with the same keys and values.

```
{} === {}
//false
```

```
{ msg: 'Hi'} === { msg: 'Hi'}
//false
```

Objects are also called reference types.

Two reference values are equal only if they refer to the same object.

```
const obj1 = {};
const obj2 = obj1;
```

```
obj1 === obj2
//true
```

Immutability

An immutable value is one that once created cannot be changed.

Primitive values are immutable. Maybe the best example is the string value. Below is an example of trying to change the character at a specific index in the string.

```
"use strict";
```

```
const text = 'ABC';
text[0] = 'a';
// Cannot assign to read only property '0' of string 'ABC'
```

Objects are mutable. Once created they can be changed. Consider the following array object.

```
const arr = ['A', 'B', 'C'];
arr[0] = 'a';
//  ["a", "B", "C"]
```

Key Notes

- Primitives are not objects, but JavaScript allows to access properties on them.
- The engine uses the wrapper functions `Number`, `BigInt`, `String`, `Boolean`, `Symbol` to create wrapper objects when accessing properties on primitives.
- The wrapper functions are also used to store the prototypes and utility functions for the corresponding primitives.
- The `null` and `undefined` primitives do not allow to access properties on them and have no associated wrapper functions.
- All values except primitives are objects, and even primitives try to look like objects.
- Objects are assigned by reference, primitives by value.
- Primitives are immutable, objects are mutable.

Chapter 15: Sets and Maps

Besides having objects that can be used as maps, JavaScript includes a more specialized class called Map, creating easier-to-manage maps. It also has a data structure for managing collections of unique values called a Set.

Sets

A set is a collection of values that does not allow duplicates and is not indexed.

Here is a set collection.

```
const set = new Set([1, 2, 3]);
//Set(3) {1, 2, 3}
```

Next is an empty set.

```
const set = new Set();
```

It can be initialized with any iterable object, even a string.

```
const set = new Set('Hello');
//Set(4) {"H", "e", "l", "o"}
```

The `size` property returns the number of elements in a set.

```
const set = new Set(['A', 'B', 'C']);
set.size;
//3
```

Elements can be added and removed from a set at any time.

```
const set = new Set();
set.add('Red');
set.add('Blue');
```

```
console.log(set);
//Set(2) {"Red", "Blue"}
```

The `delete` method removes a single element from the set.

```
set.delete('Blue');
//Set(1) {"Red"}
```

As you can see, sets are not working with indexes but with the actual values.

Unique Values

The set collection does not allow duplicates. Below is an example of trying to add the same value twice in the collection.

```
const set = new Set();
set.add('A');
set.add('A');
//Set(1) {"A"}
```

Even if we call the `add` method twice with the same value, a single `'A'` element is added to the list.

The duplicate check is done using strict equality. The number 1 and its string representation `'1'` are not equal.

```
const set = new Set();
set.add(1);
set.add('1');
//Set(2) {1, "1"}
```

Sets can be used to deal with all tasks involving duplicate values. Here is an example of removing all the duplicates from an array of numbers.

```
const arr = [1, 2, 1, 3]
const set = new Set(arr);
//Set(3) {1, 2, 3}

const newArr = Array.from(set);
//[1, 2, 3]
```

The array containing duplicates is converted into a set using the `Set` constructor. Once that is done all duplicates are removed. The set is then transformed into a new array using the `Array.from` utility. The new array of numbers has no duplicates.

Sets can be converted into an array using both `Array.from` and the spread operator. Here is a compact version for removing duplicates from an array.

```
const newArr = [...new Set([1, 2, 1, 3])];
//(3) [1, 2, 3]
```

Note that this approach works well for primitives but not for objects. Two objects having the same property name and values are not equal.

```
const set = new Set([
 { value : 1},
 { value : 1}
]);


set.size;
//2
```

The set remembers the order in which elements are added. We can loop over all the elements using the `forEach` method. The callback gets only one argument, the current value.

```
const set = new Set(['A', 'B', 'B', 'C']);
set.forEach(v => {
 console.log(v)
});
//'A'
//'B'
//'C'
```

Maps

A map is a key-value collection. Looking for a specific key has a constant `O(1)` access time.

Here is a simple translation map.

```
const map = new Map([
  ['Yes', 'Si'],
  ['No', 'No']
]);
```

```
map.get('Yes')
//'Oui'
```

Accessing a value for a specific key is done using the get(key) method.

Below is an empty map.

```
const map = new Map();
```

The argument for the Map() constructor is optional and should be an iterable object containing [key, value] arrays.

As you may remember the Object.entries returns an array of [key, value] pairs. We can use it to convert an object into a map.

```
const obj = {
  'Good Morning': 'Buongiorno',
  'Good Evening': 'Buonasera '
}
```

```
const entries = Object.entries(obj);
//[]
//["Good Morning", "Buongiorno"],
//["Good Evening", "Buonasera "]
//]
```

```
const map = new Map(entries);
//Map(2) {
//"Good Morning" => "Buongiorno",
//"Good Evening" => "Buonasera "
//}
```

Here is the compact form for transforming an object into a map.

```
new Map(Object.entries(obj));
```

The set(key, value) method allows us to edit or add a key-value pair. If the key already exists in the map it updates its value otherwise it adds a new key-value pair.

```
const map = new Map();
map.set('Hello', 'Ciao');
```

The has(key) method checks if a given key is in the map.

```
map.has('Hello')
```

```
//true
```

```
map.has('Hi')
//false
```

The `delete(key)` method removes a key and the associated value.

```
const map = new Map([
  ['Hello', 'Ciao'],
  ['Hi', 'Ciao']
]);
```

```
map.delete('Hi');
//Map(1) {"Hello" => "Ciao"}
```

The `clear` method removes all key-value pairs from the map.

```
map.clear();
```

The `size` property gives the numbers or key-value pairs.

```
const map = new Map([
  ['Apple', 'Mela'],
  ['Pear', 'Pera']
]);
```

```
map.size
//2
```

Maps can have keys of any type, not just strings. Below is an example of using boolean keys.

```
const map = new Map();
map.set(true, 'vero');
map.set(false, 'falso')
```

```
map.get(true);
//'vero'
```

The `keys` method returns an iterable object containing all the keys. The `values` method gives all the values. The `entries` method returns an iterable of `[key, value]` pairs.

```
const map = new Map([
  ['Lemon', 'Limone'],
```

```
  ['Orange', 'Arancia']
]);
```

```
[...map.keys()]
//["Lemon", "Orange"]
```

```
[...map.values()]
//  ["Limone", "Arancia"]
```

```
[...map.entries()]
//[
//["Lemon", "Limone"]
//["Orange", "Arancia"]
//]
```

We can loop over all the key-value pairs in a map using the `forEach` method.

```
map.forEach((value, key) => {
 console.log(`${key}:${value}`)
})
//'Lemon:Limone'
//'Orange:Arancia'
```

Notice that the `value` is the first argument and the `key` is the second argument for the callback function.

Key Notes

- A set is a collection of unique values.
- Sets can be used for all kinds of tasks involving unique values and removing duplicates.
- Arrays can be converted into sets using the `Set` constructor. Sets can be transformed into arrays using the `Array.from` utility or the spread operator inside the array literal.
- A map is a collection of key-value pairs. Looking for a key has a constant `O(1)` access time.
- Objects can be converted into maps using the `Map` constructor and `Object.entries` method.

Chapter 16: Objects vs Maps

Objects and maps are both dynamic collections of key-value pairs.

Starting from this definition they are pretty similar but there are some differences between them.

Construction

The object literal syntax is the simplest way to create an object map in JavaScript.

```
const gamesObj = {
  1: 'Citadels',
  2: 'Tzolkin'
};
```

Maps are created using the built-in `Map` constructor.

```
const gamesMap = new Map([
  [1, 'Citadels'],
  [2, 'Tzolkin']
]);
```

From now on I am going to use the words "objects" or "object maps" for key-value collections created using the object literal syntax and the word "maps" for maps build with the `Map` built-in constructor.

Keys

Keys on object maps are strings, while on maps, keys can be of any type.

If for example, we use a number as a key in an object literal, that number is converted to a string and used as the key.

Because the key is converted to a string we get the same result when trying to get the value for the 1 number key or for the '1' string key.

```
console.log(gamesObj[1]);
//'Citadels'
```

```
console.log(gamesObj['1']);
//'Citadels'
```

When using maps the key can be of any type so the 1 number key is different from the '1' string key.

```
gamesMap.get(1)
//'Citadels'
```

```
gamesMap.get('1')
//undefined
```

The key is unique in both cases. There cannot be two properties in an object with the same key or two entries in a map with the same key.

Unwanted Keys

Another difference is that objects have a set of unexpected key-value pairs inherited from the Object.prototype.

When we print the Object.prototype we can see it has a few properties like hasOwnProperty, isPrototypeOf, toLocaleString, toString.

```
console.log(Object.prototype);
```

An object created with the object's literal syntax has all these properties on it. So the empty object {} is not really empty. Check the code below.

```
const mapObject = {};
console.log(mapObject['toString']);
//f toString() { [native code] }
```

We created an "empty object" and we are able to access the toString key on it.

A better option for creating object maps is to use the Object.create(null) utility.

```
const mapObject = Object.create(null);

console.log(mapObject['toString']);
//undefined
```

`Object.create(null)` builds an object with no prototype.

Order of Key-Value Pairs

The original order of the key-value pairs is preserved in maps, while in objects it is not.

```
const gamesObj = {
  2: 'Tzolkin',
  1: 'Citadels',
};

const keys = Object.keys(gamesObj);
//["1", "2"];

const keyValuePairs = Object.entries(gamesObj);
//["1", "Citadels"]
//["2", "Tzolkin"]
```

Notice that when the object is created the key 2 comes before the key 1. When retrieving all the entries 2 comes after 1.

Below is a similar collection built with the `Map` constructor. This time the initial order is preserved.

```
const gamesMap = new Map([
  [2, 'Tzolkin'],
  [1, 'Citadels']
])

const keys = gamesMap.keys();
//MapIterator {2, 1}

const keyValuePairs = gamesMap.entries();
//MapIterator {2 => "Tzolkin", 1 => "Citadels"}
```

Interface Methods

Getting

Accessing properties on an object is done using the dot or the bracket notation. In our case because the initial key is a number we can only use the bracket notation.

```
gamesObj[1];
//'Citadels'
```

On maps, we can retrieve a value using the get(key) method.

```
gamesMap.get(1);
//'Citadels'
```

Checking for Keys

Checking if a key is already in a map is done using the has(key) method.

```
gamesMap.has(1);
//true

gamesMap.get(3);
//false
```

On objects, we can use the hasOwnProperty method to check for a key.

The hasOwnProperty method verifies if the object has the specified own property.

```
gamesObj.hasOwnProperty(1);
//true
```

Adding

Adding a new key-value pair on a map is done using the set(key, value) method.

```
gamesMap.set(3, 'Catan');
//{1=>'Citadels', 2=>'Tzolkin', 3=>'Catan'}
```

Again for objects, we use the bracket or the dot notation for adding new properties.

```
gamesObj[3] = 'Catan';
//{ 1: 'Citadels', 2: 'Tzolkin', 3: 'Catan'};
```

Deleting

Maps have the `delete(key)` method for deleting pairs.

```
gamesMap.delete(1);
```

On objects, we can use the `delete` operator.

```
delete gamesObl[1];
```

Reading the size

Maps keep their size updated so we can get the size using the `size` property.

```
console.log(gamesMap.size);
```

Here is how we can test for emptiness on a map.

```
gamesMap.size === 0
```

Objects do not have a specific method for getting the size. We need to use external helper functions like `Object.keys()`.

```
const size = Object.keys(gamesObj).length;
console.log(size);
```

Looping

We can iterate over the entries in a map using the `forEach` method.

```
const gamesMap = new Map([
  [1, 'Citadels'],
  [2, 'Tzolkin']
]);

gamesMap.forEach((value, key)=>{
  console.log(`${key} - ${value}`)
});
//1 - Citadels
//2 - Tzolkin
```

Objects require helpers functions for accessing the key-values pairs.

`Object.entries` returns an array of `[key, value]` pairs with all the owned properties of an object. Once we have that we can use the array methods likes `forEach`.

```
const gamesObj = {
  1: 'Citadels',
  2: 'Tzolkin'
};

Object
  .entries(gamesObj)
  .forEach(([key, value])=>{
    console.log(`${key} - ${value}`)
  });
//1 - Citadels
//2 - Tzolkin
```

JSON Support

The JSON utility works for objects but not for maps.

```
const gamesObj = {
  1: 'Citadels',
  2: 'Tzolkin'
};

const json = JSON.stringify(gamesObj);
//{"1":"Citadels","2":"Tzolkin"}
```

Maps do not work with JSON.stringify utility. Serializing results in an empty object.

```
const gamesMap = new Map([
  [1, 'Citadels'],
  [2, 'Tzolkin']
]);

const json = JSON.stringify(gamesMap);
//{}
```

Key Notes

- Objects in JavaScript are what in other languages are called hash maps. Accessing keys on the map object has an O(1) access time, meaning that it takes a constant time to get the key, no matter the amount of data in the object map.

- No matter how these key-value collections are created using the `Map` constructor or the object literal syntax they are mainly used for fast searching data. Both of them perform in `O(1)` access time. Retrieving a key does not require scanning through all of the data.
- Maps offer a nicer interface for managing the key-value pairs. In scenarios that require adding and removing entries, Map is a better choice.
- When creating a key-value collection once and use it to search for keys an object map can be enough.

Chapter 17: Null and Undefined

`null` and `undefined` are the nullish values.

They are the only primitive values that don't look like objects. They don't allow accessing properties. Trying to do that results in an error.

undefined

`undefined` represents a not initialized variable.

Below is an example of a variable that is not initialized. It gets the value of `undefined`.

```
let x;
console.log(x);
//undefined
```

Variables declared with `const` should be initialized. The previous case can happen only when declaring variables with `let` and `var`.

Trying to access a property that does not exist on an object results in `undefined`.

```
const book = {};
```

```
book.title
//undefined
```

The same happens when trying to retrieve an element that does not exist on an array. It does not throw an exception, but it returns `undefined`.

```
const arr = [];
```

```
console.log(arr[0]);
//undefined
```

Remember that arrays are emulated using objects.

When a function is invoked with fewer arguments than it takes the remaining parameters are initialized with **undefined**.

```
function doSomething(x){
  console.log(x);
}


doSomething();
//undefined
```

If a function does not explicitly return a value it returns **undefined**.

```
function doSomething() {}


console.log(doSomething());
//undefined
```

If the **return** statement is used but without any value after it, the function still returns **undefined**.

```
function doSomething(no){
  if(no === 1){
    return;
  }

  return 0;
}


console.log(doSomething(1));
//undefined
```

Accessing a property using the optional chaining operator (?.) on **undefined** results in **undefined**.

```
console.log(undefined?.name);
//undefined
```

The **undefined** is a falsy value. The check evaluates to **false** when using the conditional operator for example.

```
undefined ? true : false;
```

```
//false
```

The type of `undefined` is `'undefined'`.

```
typeof undefined
//'undefined'
```

null

`null` represents the intentional absence of an object value.

```
let selectedBook = null;
```

We can create an object with no prototype using the `null` value.

```
const map = Object.create(null);
```

Accessing a property using optional chaining operator on `null` results in `undefined`.

```
console.log(null?.name);
//undefined
```

The `typeof` operator wrongly returns `'object'` as the type of `null`.

```
typeof null
//'object'
```

Nullish Coalescing Operator

The nullish coalescing operator (**??**) checks the left-side expression and if that is nullish it returns the right-side expression , otherwise, it returns the left-side expression.

The nullish coalescing operator lets us define a default value. In the next example, the left-side value is nullish so it returns the right-side value `"default"`.

```
const value = null;
const newValue = value ?? "default";
//"default"
```

In the following case, the left-side value is not nullish so it returns that value, 0.

```
const value = 0;
const newValue = value ?? "default";
```

```
console.log(newValue);
//0
```

The logical operator Or (||) does a similar thing, only that it checks for falsy, not nullish values.

```
const value = 0;
const newValue = value || "default";
console.log(newValue);
//"default"
```

The left-side value is falsy so the Or operator (||) results in the right-side value.

Optional Chaining Operator

Before discussing the optional chaining operator (?.) let's look at an example of accessing properties of an object.

Consider the following book object.

```
const book = {
    name: 'JavaScript The Good Parts',
    author: {
      name: 'Douglas Crockford'
    }
  };
```

We can access the author's name using the dot notation.

```
console.log(book.author.name);
//'Douglas Crockford'
```

However, when trying to access the author's name using the same syntax on a book that does not have an author we get an error.

```
const book = {
    name: 'How JavaScript Works'
};

console.log(book.author.name);
//Cannot read property 'name' of undefined
```

The optional chaining operator (?.) permits reading the value of a property located within a chain of objects. The (?.) operator results in `undefined` when a property is nullish. It allows us to access chained properties even when some references may be missing.

When the `author` property is nullish the optional chaining operator results in `undefined`.

```
const book = {
    name: 'How JavaScript Works'
};


console.log(book.author?.name);
//undefined
```

When the `author` property is available we get its name.

Key Notes

- `null` and `undefined` are the only nullish values. They are not treated as objects so we cannot access properties on them.
- Reading a variable or parameter that is not initialized results in `undefined`
- Accessing a missing property of an object gives `undefined`.
- `null` expresses the intentional absence of an object
- When the first operand is not nullish the nullish coalescing operator (`??`) returns the first operand and the second is not evaluated. When the first operand is nullish, then it returns the second operand. It is similar to the Or operator(`||`) only that it checks for nullish values instead of falsy values.
- The optional chaining operator (`?.`) is similar to the chaining operator (`.`) but instead of throwing an error if a reference is nullish it short-circuits the evaluation and returns `undefined`.

Chapter 18: Variables Declarations

There are three ways for declaring variables in JavaScript. We are going to discuss all and look at the differences between them.

var

The `var` statement was the initial way for declaring variables but has become obsolete.

It is optional to initialize the `var` variables. An uninitialized variable stores the `undefined` value.

```
var name;

console.log(name);
//undefined
```

When declaring a variable with `var` inside a function that variable is available everywhere in the function.

Variables declared with `var` have no block scope. Consider the next example.

```
{
    var name = 'Jon Snow';
}

console.log(name);
//'Jon Snow';
```

Variables declared with `var` are hoisted to the top of their scope, being that a function or a module, and as such, they can be accessed before the declaration. In that case, they have the value of undefined.

A module is a file basically in JavaScript.

```
console.log(name);
//undefined

var name = 'Jon Snow';
```

Because var variables have no block scope they may cause some confusion like in the next example. Developers familiar with languages where variables have block scope may be confused that the second declaration inside a block reassigns the previous variable and does not create a new one.

```
var name = 'Eddard Stark'
{
    var name = 'Robb Stark';
}

console.log(name);
//'Robb Stark'
```

The redeclaration of the same variable in the same scope using var does not throw an error but just updates the already declared variable.

```
var name = 'Eddard Stark'
var name = 'Robb Stark';

console.log(name);
//'Robb Stark'
```

Nevertheless, var variables have function scope. Consider the following example where the name variable is declared inside a module and also inside a function.

```
var name = 'Tywin Lannister';

function process(){
    var name = 'Tyrion Lannister';
}
```

Once we declare a variable with the same name in a function we don't have access to the variable from the outside module with the same name.

The variable declared inside the function is local to that function and does not interfere with the module variable having the same name.

As already said `var` has become obsolete, so don't worry too much about the confusion it creates.

let

The `let` statement declares variables that can have block scope. Once declared in a block they are only visible inside that block. Check the example below.

```
{
    let name = 'Jon Snow';
}
```

```
console.log(name);
//ReferenceError: name is not defined
```

We can also declare several variables with a single `let` statement.

```
let firstName = 'Jon', lastName = 'Snow';
```

Declaring variables with the same name both outside and inside a block creates two distinct variables. Once we do that, in the scope of a block we don't longer have access to the variable with the same name from outside that block.

```
let name = 'Eddard Stark'
{
    let name = 'Robb Stark';
}
```

```
console.log(name);
//'Eddard Stark'
```

As with `var`, it is optional to initialize the `let` variables.

```
let name;
```

```
console.log(name);
//undefined
```

We can no longer use a variable before declaring it. Check the next example.

```
console.log(name);
//ReferenceError: Cannot access 'name' before initialization

let name = 'Daenerys Targaryen';
```

Also, we cannot redeclare a variable in the same scope. Doing that throws an error. This is fine because it was confusing to allow such behavior.

```
let name = 'Cersei Lannister';
let name = 'Cersei Baratheon';
//SyntaxError: Identifier 'name' has already been declared
```

const

The const statement declares variables that cannot be reassigned.

```
const name = 'A Game of Thrones';
name = 'A Clash of Kings';
//TypeError: Assignment to constant variable.
```

const variables have block scope. The next two const declarations create two independent variables.

```
const name = 'Eddard Stark'
{
    const name = 'Robb Stark';
}

console.log(name);
//'Eddard Stark'
```

Be aware that we deal with "real constants" only when values are immutable. A string is an immutable value, so next is an example of a "true constant".

```
const castle = 'Casterly Rock';
```

Objects are not immutable, on the contrary. The following variable can be changed even if it is declared with const.

```
const castle = { name : 'Casterly Rock' };

castle.name = 'Winterfell';
console.log(castle);
//{name: "Winterfell"}
```

In order to create a "real constant", we need to freeze the object.

```
const castle = Object.freeze({
  name : 'Casterly Rock'
  });
```

```
castle.name = 'Winterfell';
//Cannot assign to read only property 'name' of object
```

Destructuring Assignment

The destructuring assignment syntax allows unpacking values from arrays, or properties from objects, into new variables.

The syntax is similar to the array or the object literals only that is on the left side of the assignment operator.

Array Destructuring

Consider the following array.

```
const arr = [1, 2, 3]
```

Below is an example of extracting all these values from the array into three variables.

```
const [a, b, c] = arr;

console.log(a); //1
console.log(b); //2
console.log(c); //3
```

a, b, c are three constants declared with the `const` statement and initialized using the destructuring assignment syntax.

We can separate the variable declaration from assigning its value via destructuring. Below is an example.

```
const arr = [1, 2, 3];
let a, b, c;
[a, b, c] = [1, 2, 3];

console.log(a); //1
console.log(b); //2
console.log(c); //3
```

Nonetheless, the most common use case is to do both the declaration and initialized of the variables on the same line when using the destructuring assignment syntax.

There is no need to extract all the values from the array. We can for example extract only the first two values. The extra values on the right side of the assignment operator are ignored.

```
const arr = [1, 2, 3];
const [a, b] = arr;
```

We can also define more variables than the number of values available in the array. The extra variables on the left side are set to **undefined**. Here is an example.

```
const [a, b, c] = [1, 2];
console.log(a); //1
console.log(b); //2
console.log(c); //undefined
```

When we expect fewer values in the array than the number of variables a better idea is to use default values. Below is an example of setting a default for a variable in the destructuring assignment syntax. When the value is missing on the right side, the variable is set to the default value.

```
const [a, b, c = 0] = [1, 2]
console.log(a); //1
console.log(b); //2
console.log(c); //0
```

When destructuring an array, we can assign the remaining part of it to a variable using the rest pattern.

Below is an example of extracting the first value from the array into a variable and assigning the remaining values into another variable holding a new array.

```
const [a, ...newArr] = [1, 2, 3];

console.log(a); // 1
console.log(newArr); // [2, 3]
```

The destructuring syntax makes it easy to return two or more values from a function. We just return an array with all the values and then use the destructuring syntax to assigned those values to new variables. Here is an example.

```
function getValues(){
    const v1 = 1;
    const v2 = 2;
    return [v1, v2];
}

const [a, b] = getValues();
console.log(a); //1
console.log(b); //2
```

Object Destructuring

Consider the following object.

```
const point = { x: 1, y: 2};
```

We can extract out the two properties into two variables having the same names.

```
const {x, y} = point;

console.log(x); //1
console.log(y); //2
```

There is no need to extract all the properties from an object. The remaining properties are just ignored. Below is an example.

```
const { x } = point;

console.log(x); //1
```

We can also try to extract properties that are missing from the object. The variable missing a matching property is assigned to **undefined**.

```
const { x, z } = point;

console.log(x); //1
console.log(z); //undefined
```

It is a better idea to define default values when the related property may be missing from the destructured object. Below is an example.

```
const { x, z = 0 } = point;
```

```
console.log(x); //1
console.log(z); //0
```

We can also destructure properties into variables with different names. Here is an example.

```
const point = { x: 1, y: 2};
const { x : xAxis, y: yAxis } = point;

console.log(xAxis); //1
console.log(yAxis); //2
```

The xAxis variable is assigned to the x property from the point object and the yAxis variable is assigned to the y property.

Key Notes

- var cannot have block scope. let and const can have block scope.
- var are hoisted to the top of their scope and can be accessed before the declaration. let and const variables cannot be accessed before the declaration.
- var and let variables can be reassigned. const variables cannot be reassigned.
- const variable must be initialized when declaring. Initializing var and let variables is optional. If not initialized they store the undefined value.
- The destructuring assignment syntax allows extracting values from arrays and objects into new variables.

Chapter 19: Statements

JavaScript has as we have seen three stamens for declaring variables var, let and cost. It has two conditional statements and several loop statements.

Conditional Statements

if and switch are the conditional statements.

if

The if statement executes a block of code when the given condition is truthy.

Here is an example. Note that any kind of value can be used as the condition.

```
const value = NaN;

if(Number.isNaN(value)){
  console.log('NaN');
}
//'NaN'
```

The if/else statement executes the first block of code when the given condition is truthy otherwise it runs the else-block of code.

```
const value = 1.2;

if(Number.isInteger(value)){
  console.log('Integer');
} else {
  console.log('Not an Integer');
```

```
}
//'Not an Integer'
```

switch

The `switch` statement selects a block of code to be executed base on a given expression. The value of the expression is compared with the values of each case block. When one is found the associated block of code is executed otherwise the default block is run if there is one.

The `default` keyword defines the default block to be executed when there is no case match. There can only be only one default block. Even if it is optional it is recommended to have the default block.

```
const action = 'INCREMENT';

switch(action){
  case 'INCREMENT':
    console.log('INCREMENT');
  break;
  case 'DECREMENT':
    console.log('INCREMENT');
  break;
  default:
    console.log('DEFAULT');
}
```

The `break` keyword exits the `switch` block. When the `break` is omitted, the next code block in the `switch` statement runs.

There is no need to have the `break` statement when using `return`. Here is an example of a function handling actions and returning a new value.

```
function doAction(action, value){
  switch(action){
    case 'INCREMENT':
      return value + 1
    case 'DECREMENT':
      return value - 1;
    default:
      return value;
  }
}
```

```
doAction('INCREMENT', 0);
//1
```

Loop Statements

There are five loop statements in the language `while`, `do/while`, `for`, `for/in` and `for/of`.

Loops can be used to execute the same block of code a number of times.

for

`for` executes of a block of code a number of times and increments while a condition is truthy

The next loop computes the sum of the first three numbers.

```
let sum = 0;
for(i = 1; i <= 3; i++){
  sum = sum + i;
}
```

```
console.log(sum);
//6
```

The loop can be read as follows:

- `sum` gets initialized with 0
- The loop starts and `i` is initialized with 1.
- The condition is evaluated 1 <= 3 so the loop continues. The `sum` is changed to 0 + 1, and `i` is incremented i = 2.
- The condition is evaluated 2 <= 3 so the loop continues. A new iteration starts with `sum` = 1 and `i` = 2. The `sum` is changed to 1 + 2, and `i` is incremented i = 3.
- The condition is evaluated 3 <= 3 so the loop continues. A new iteration starts with `sum` = 3 and `i` = 3. The `sum` is changed to 3 + 3, and `i` is incremented i = 4.
- The condition is evaluated 4 <= 3 so the loop stops.

for/in

`for/in` loops through the properties of an object

```
const flight = {
  no: 815,
  from: 'Sydney',
  to: 'Los Angeles'
}

for (key in flight) {
  console.log(key)
}
//'no'
//'from'
//'to'
```

When used on an array we get all the string indexes. As you remember arrays are emulated using objects. The type of the index variable is 'string'.

```
const letters = ['A', 'B', 'C'];

for (index in letters) {
  console.log(index);
}
//'0'
//'1'
//'2'
```

for/of

for/of loops through the values of an iterable object

An iterable object is one that can be iterated over. Arrays, sets, maps are all iterable, even strings are iterable. It means we can use the for-of statement to loop over all of them.

```
for(const value of [1,2,3]){
  console.log(value);
}
//1
//2
//3

for(const value of new Set([1,2,3])){
  console.log(value);
```

```
}
//1
//2
//3

const map = new Map();
map.set(1, 'A');
map.set(2, 'B');
for(const value of map){
  console.log(value);
}
//[1, 'A']
//[2, 'B']

for(const value of 'ABC'){
  console.log(value);
}
//'A'
//'B'
//'C'
```

while

`while` executes a block of code while a specified condition is truthy

Next, is a condition in the while-loop checking a number. When the number is 0 the loop stops because 0 is evaluated to `false` and all the other numbers are evaluated to `true`.

```
let i = 3, sum = 0;

while(i){
  sum = sum + i;
  i = i - 1 ;
}

console.log(sum);
//6
```

The loop can be read as follows:

- sum is initialized with 0, i with 3

- i is 3 which is truthy so the loop continues. sum is updated to 0 + 3, i is decremented and becomes 2
- i is 2 which is truthy so the loop continues. sum is updated to 3 + 2, i is decremented and becomes 1
- i is 1 which is truthy so the loop continues. sum is updated to 5 + 1, i is decremented and becomes 0
- i is 0 which is falsy. The loop stops.

do/while

do/while executes a block of code while a specified condition is truthy

The while statement tests the condition at the beginning of the loop, and if the condition is truthy the block of code is executed. The do/while statement tests the condition at the end of the loop, meaning that it executes the block of code at least once.

Semicolons

Semicolons are used to separate statements. Below is an example.

```
const x = 1;
const y = 2;
```

However, they can be omitted when statements are written on separate lines.

```
const x = 1
const y = 2
```

When the statements are written on the same line the semicolons are required.

```
const x = 1; const y = 2;
```

JavaScript has an automatic semicolon insertion mechanism that tries to correct the program.

Be aware of the consequence of adding a semicolon to the end of the return or throw statements. Consider the next code.

```
function getGameObject(){
  return
    { name: 'Fornite'};
}
```

You may think that this function returns an object, but it doesn't. It returns **undefined**.

```
console.log(getGameObject());
```

The automatic semicolon mechanism tries to put a semicolon at the end of the **return** line, sees that is a valid code and puts it. The previous code is equivalent to:

```
function getGameObject(){
  return;
    { name: 'Fornite'};
}
```

To avoid this issue, put the first curly brace **{** on the same line as the **return** statement:

```
function getGameObject(){
  return {
    name: 'Fornite'
  };
}
```

```
console.log(getGameObject());
//{name: "Fornite"}
```

The same caution should be taken for primitive values. The following code is interpreted as **return**; 1; and the result is **undefined**.

```
return
1
```

Primitive values should be returned on the same line.

```
return 1;
return "Hello"
return true;
```

```
throw "There was an error";
```

Key Notes

- The `if` statement executes a block of code when the condition is truthy.
- The `if/else` has an else-block that is executed when the condition is falsy.
- The `switch` statement selects a block of code to be executed base on a given expression.
- The `for` statement allows processing arrays one element at a time.
- The `while` and `do/while` are generic loop statements. There is one difference between them, the `while` statement checks the condition before doing an iteration and `do/while` tests it after doing an iteration.

Chapter 20: Dynamic Typing

Variables can store values of different types and they inherit the type of their values. As such variables can change their type.

Values don't change their type.

0 is always a number.

'' is always a string.

{} is always an object.

function(){} is always a function.

```
typeof 1    //number
typeof ''   //string
typeof {}   //object
typeof function(){}   //function
```

For example, the following variable is of type **number** because the type of the value 1 is **number**.

```
let x = 1;

typeof 1;
//'number'

typeof x;
//'number'
```

However, we can store a new value of type **bigint** in the same variable.

```
x = 1n;
```

```
typeof 1n;
//'bigint'
```

```
typeof x;
//'bigint'
```

const

Variables declared with `const` cannot be resigned and as such, they cannot change their type. Only variables declared with `var` and `let` can change their type.

```
const x = 1;
typeof x;
//'number'
```

```
x = '';
//Uncaught TypeError: Assignment to constant variable.
```

Object Properties

Properties can store values of any type.

`typeof` may be used to check the type of property.

```
const obj = { x: 1 };
```

```
typeof obj.x
//number
```

Nonetheless, the value of the property can change and so its type. A frozen object cannot be changed and as such its properties cannot change their type.

The `Object.freeze` utility can freeze an object.

```
"use strict";
const obj = Object.freeze({
  x: 1
});
```

```
typeof obj.x
//number
```

```
obj.x = 2n;
//Cannot assign to read only property 'x' of object
```

Parameters

Parameters accept values of all types.

Below is an example of calling the `log` function three times with different arguments. The first time the argument is of type number, then is a string, and in the last call is an object.

```
function log(x){
  console.log(x);
}

log(1);
log('one');
log({value : 1});
```

Array Values

The values in arrays can be of any type. Here is an example.

```
const arr = [1, '2', '3'];
```

However, we can convert it to an array of strings or numbers using the `String` or the `Number` built-in functions together with the `map` array method.

```
arr.map(Number);
//[1, 2, 3]

arr.map(String);
//["1", "2", "3"]
```

Key Notes

- Variables declared with `let` and `var` can change their type.
- Variables declared with `const` cannot change their type.
- Properties can have values of all types. Frozen objects cannot change the type of their properties.
- Function parameters accept values of any type.

- Values in an array can be of any type. We can use the `map` method and the built-in functions like `Number` or `String` to convert it into an array of numbers or strings.

Chapter 21: Exceptions

There are cases when functions fail due to an unexpected problem. A common practice is to throw exceptions in these situations and have a part of the code handling them.

The JavaScript language throws exceptions. For example, trying to change a frozen object results in an exception. Here is an example.

```
"use strict";
const obj = Object.freeze({});

obj.msg = "Hi";
//Uncaught TypeError:
//Cannot add property msg, object is not extensible
```

Execution Stops

The execution of the current function stops when an error is thrown. The statements after that are not executed.

Consider the next example trying to access a property on null. The code stops after the exception is thrown. The last two lines from the following code are not executed.

```
const obj = null;
const name = obj.name;
//Uncaught TypeError: Cannot read property 'name' of null

const text = `Name: ${name}`;
console.log(name);
```

throw

Besides the errors raised by the language, we can create custom exceptions.

Exceptions are raised using the `throw` statement.

```
throw "This is an error"
```

We can throw basically any value.

```
throw 1
throw {
  code : 1,
  message: 'User not authorized'
}
```

A better idea is to throw objects created with the `Error` constructor

```
throw new Error("This was an error")
```

Below is another example of raising a custom exception. The `divide` function throws a custom error if the divisor parameter is 0.

```
function divide(no, divisor){
  if(divisor === 0){
    throw new Error("Division by zero error")
  }

  return no / divisor;
}

divide(1, 0);
//Division by zero error
```

try/catch

The `try` statement wraps a block of code and defines an exception handler in the `catch` close.

The `try` and `catch` statements come in pairs.

Here is an example of handling an exception thrown by the language when trying to change an immutable string.

```
"use strict";
```

```
try {
  let text ="aBC";
  text[0] = "A";
}
catch(e){
  const { message } = e
  console.log(message)
}
//Cannot assign to read only property '0' of string 'aBC'
```

Trying to parse in invalid JSON string results in an exception being raised.

```
JSON.parse('');
//Uncaught SyntaxError: Unexpected end of JSON input
```

The control is passed to the first `catch` block in the call stack. If no `catch` block exists in the caller functions, the execution ends.

In the next example, the `try`/`catch` block is used to detect if a string is a valid JSON and return a boolean.

```
function isValidJSON(text){
  try {
    JSON.parse(text);
    return true;
  }
  catch(e) {
    return false;
  }
}

console.log(isValidJSON(''));
//false

console.log(isValidJSON('{}'));
//true
```

Rethrowing an Exception

We can use `throw` statement and rethrow an exception after catching it. In the following example, we catch the exception, log it into the console, and then re-throw it.

```
function process(){
```

```
  throw new Error("Could not transform");
}

try {
  process();
}
catch(e){
  const errorMessage = `Exception: ${e.message}`;
  console.log(errorMessage);
  throw e;
}
//Exception: Could not transform
//Uncaught Error: Could not transform
```

finally

The `finally` statement allows us to execute a piece of logic despite the result of the `try`/`catch` block.

Consider the next example where the code execution stops when the error is thrown. The console timer is not stoped and the duration of the process is not shown.

```
function process(){
  throw new Error("Could not transform");
}

console.time("duration");
process();
console.timeEnd("duration");
//Uncaught Error: Could not transform
```

The `console.time` utility starts a timer in the console. It allows us to measure the duration of operations. The `console.timeEnd` function ends the timer and displays the result in the console.

Both utilities can take a name as a parameter and allow us to have several timers on the page each having different names.

The next example uses the `finally` block to end the timer and log the duration of processing the call whether or not an exception is thrown.

```
function process(){
  throw new Error("Could not transform");
```

```
}

console.time("duration");
try{
  process();
}
finally{
  console.timeEnd("duration");
}
```

```
//duration: 0.030029296875 ms
//Uncaught Error: Could not transform
```

The `finally` block is usually used to clean up resources.

Key Notes

- The execution of the current function ends when an error is thrown.
- Custom exceptions are raised using the `throw` statement.
- We can throw basically any type of value but a better approach is to throw objects created with the **Error** constructor.
- The `try/catch` statement wraps a block of code and specifies a handler in case an exception is thrown.
- The `finally` block lets us execute a piece of logic, after the `try/catch` block, regardless of the result.

Chapter 22: Closures

What is a closure?

Before answering this question we need to first acknowledge that in JavaScript functions can be defined inside other functions. Below is such an example.

```
function outer(){
  function inner(){}
}
```

As you can see the **inner** function is created inside the **outer** function.

Not only that we can defined functions inside other functions but the inner function can access variables and parameters from the outer function. Let's extend the previous example.

```
function outer(){
  const x = 1;
  function inner(){
    console.log(x);
  }
}
```

The **inner** function accesses the x variable from the **outer** function.

Moreover, the inner function has the ability to access variables and parameters from the outer function even after the outer function has been executed.

```
function outer(){
  const x = 1;
  return function inner(){
    console.log(x);
```

```
  }
}
```

```
const log = outer();
log(); //1
log(); //1
```

As you notice the outer function is executed but the x variable is not destroyed. The x variable is alive as long as the inner function lives.

When the inner function is eligible for garbage collection then the x variable is also eligible for garbage collection.

Closure

Knowing all these we can now define what a closure is.

Closure is the ability of a function to access and more important to remember the variables from the outer scope. The outer scope is usually a function as you have seen but it can be also a block scope, a module. A function with such an ability is called a closure.

Remembering the variables from the outer scope is very important. Consider the next example using the setTimeout. The inner function is a closure accessing the variable x from the outer function. Image what it means if after 4 seconds when the inner function is called, it has no access the x variable anymore because the outer function has finished its execution.

```
function outer(){
  const x = 1;
  setTimeout(function inner(){
    console.log(x);
  }, 4000);
}
```

```
outer();
//1 after 4s
```

Nonetheless, in JavaScript variables referred to by closures are not destroyed until the closure itself is destroyed.

Below is an example of creating a similar closure referring to a parent block scope. As you can see the outer scope is not necessarily a function.

```
{
  const x = 1;
  setTimeout(function inner(){
    console.log(x);
  }, 4000);
}
//1 after 4s
```

It is most probable that you have already used closure without paying too much attention to it.

Encapsulation

What is interesting is that we can create encapsulation this way. Encapsulation means hiding information.

Consider the next example.

```
function createRateIt(){
  const ratings = [];

  return function(rating){
    if(rating){
      ratings.push(rating);
    }

    const total = ratings.reduce((x, y) => x + y);
    return total / ratings.length;
  }
}

const rateIt = createRateIt();
rateIt(5);
rateIt(3);
rateIt(4);

const avgRating = rateIt();
//4
```

The `createRateIt` function returns the inner function.

Notice that the inner function has access to the `ratings` parameter from the outer function. It remembers this parameter even after `createRateIt` parent function has been executed. The `rateIt` function is a closure.

The `ratings` data is hidden.

Closures encapsulate data. The `ratings` array is encapsulated inside the `rateIt` closure function and it cannot be accessed directly from the outside. It can be changed only by using the `rateIt` closure function.

Key Notes

- Functions can be declared inside other functions and can have access to variables and parameters from the outer functions.
- More important is that inner functions have access to these variables and parameters even after the outer functions have been executed.
- Closure is the ability of a function to access and more important to remember the variables and parameters from the outer scope.
- An inner function that has access to variables and parameters from the scope in which it is created, even after the outer scope finishes its execution, is called a closure.

Chapter 23: Scope of a Variable

A variable in JavaScript can have global, module, function, or block scope. We are going to analyze all of them.

Scope refers to both the visibility and the lifetime of a variable.

Global Scope

Variables defined in the global scope are visible everywhere in the application.

When there is no module system enabled inside the application, variables declared outside functions are global variables.

JavaScript has what is called the global object. When the application starts a new global object is created.

In the browser, `window` was used to refer to the global object. The `globalThis` is the new standard way of referring to the global object.

```
window === globalThis
//true
```

All global functions like `Number`, `String`, `Boolean`, `setTimeout`, constants like `NaN` or `Infinity`, or global objects like `Math` and `JSON` are added as properties on this object.

```
globalThis.hasOwnProperty('NaN')
//true
```

```
globalThis.hasOwnProperty('Number')
//true
```

```
globalThis.hasOwnProperty('setTimeout')
//true
```

```
globalThis.hasOwnProperty('Math')
//true
```

All global variables defined with `var` are added as properties on the global object.

```
var numberArr = [1, 2, 3];
console.log(globalThis.numberArr);
//[1, 2, 3]
```

Global variables created with `const` and `let` are not added as properties on this object.

```
const numberArr = [1, 2, 3];
```

```
globalThis.numberArr
//undefined
```

```
globalThis.hasOwnProperty('numberArr')
//false
```

Declaring properties on the global object creates global variables.

```
globalThis.numberArr = [1, 2, 3];
console.log(numberArr);
//[1, 2, 3]
```

Most of the current applications have a module system enabled. Declaring a variable inside a module does not create a global variable.

Module Scope

A variable declared inside a module, outside any function or block scope, is available inside that module but it is not accesible to other modules unless it is explicitly exported.

A module is a file in JavaScript.

In order to make a variable or a function available to the other modules, we need to export it. There are two kinds of exports, named and default.

Named Exports

There can be multiple named exports per module.

Consider the `actions.js` file module exporting two constants.

```
const add_todo = 'add_todo';
const remove_todo = 'remove_todo';

export { add_todo, remove_todo };
```

To have access to functions or variables from other modules in the current module, we have to first import them.

Below is an example of importing the two constants from the `actions.js` module. When using named exports we have to specify the same names as the ones used in the export.

```
import { add_todo, remove_todo } from './actions';

console.log(add_todo);
//'add_todo'
```

Nonetheless, we can rename an export when importing it. The next example imports the `add_todo` constant but inserts it with the `addTodo` name into the current module.

```
import { add_todo as addTodo } from './actions';

console.log(addTodo);
//'add_todo'
```

We can import all the exports from a module and insert a module object containing all of them. Once we do that we need to use the module name to access a specific export. In next example `actions` is the module object containing all the exports and is used to access the `add_todo` constant.

```
import * as actions from './actions';

console.log(actions.add_todo);
//'add_todo'
```

Default Export

A module allows several named exports but only one default export.

Below is an example of a default export.

```
function square(x) {
  return x * x;
}

export default square;
```

In others scripts, the default export can be imported with any name.

```
import computeSquare from './square';

computeSquare(3);
//97
```

Function Scope

Variables declared inside a function outside any block or inner function are visible everywhere inside that function.

Function scope means that parameters and variables defined in a function are visible within the function, but are not accessible outside of the function.

`var` variables and parameters a visible everywhere inside the function.

`let` and `const` variables are visible in the function only after their declaration. When declared at the top of the function they are visible everywhere inside the function.

In the following example, we can notice that the x variable is visible only inside the doTask function.

```
function doTask(){
  let x = 1;
  console.log(x);
}

doTask();
//1

console.log(x);
//Uncaught ReferenceError: x is not defined
```

Block Scope

A variable declared inside a block is visible only within that block.

Block scope is defined with curly braces.

Only variables declared with let and const can have block scope.

```
{
  const x = 1;
}
console.log(x);
//Uncaught ReferenceError: x is not defined
```

Lexical Scope

Lexical scope means that a child scope has access to the variables and parameters from their parent scopes.

For instance, we can define a function inside another function. The inner function has access to variables and parameters from the outer function.

```
function outer(){
  const x = 1;

  function inner(){
    console.log(x);
  }

  inner();
}

outer();
//1
```

We may also define an inner function inside another function that is also an inner function itself. Here is an example.

```
function secondOuter(){
  const x = 1;

  function firstOuter(){
    function inner(){
      console.log(x);
```

```
    }
    inner();
  }
  firstOuter();
}

secondOuter();
//1
```

The `inner` function has access to the x variable from the `secondOuter` scope which is not its direct parent scope. `firstOuter` is the parent scope of the `inner` function and `secondOuter` scope is the direct parent of the `firstOuter` scope.

We can also define blocks inside other blocks. The inner block has access to variables from the outer blocks.

```
{
  const x = 1;
  {
    {
      console.log(x);
    }
  }
}
//1
```

What we have actually created so far are nested scopes.

Lexical scoping defines how variables are resolved in nested scopes, usually nested functions. The inner scopes have access to variables and parameters from the parent scopes even if the parent scopes have exited.

Lexical scope gives the inner scope the ability to access variables and parameters from the outer scope in which it is defined and more important to remember those variables and parameters even after the parent scopes have exited.

Every scope has a link to the parent scope. This creates a scope chain. At the end of the chain is the global scope. When a variable is used, JavaScript looks down the scope chain until it either finds the requested variable or until it reaches the global scope, which is the end of the scope chain.

Lexical scope makes possible closure functions. The outer scope where a closure is created can be a function, a module, or a block.

Strict Mode

Strict mode is enabled by adding "use strict"; at the beginning of a script file or a function.

The default, the non-strict mode is sometimes called the sloppy mode.

The strict mode fixes several JavaScript issues.

In the sloppy mode assigning a value to a variable that was not declared creates a global variable. Below is an example of a function creating a global variable by missing the variable declaration.

```
function doSomething() {
  x = 1;
}

doSomething();
console.log(x);
//1
```

The strict mode does not allow using a variable without declaring it.

When "use strict"; is used at the beginning of a script file it affects all the code in the script.

```
"use strict";
function doSomething() {
  x = 1;
}

doSomething();
//Uncaught ReferenceError: x is not defined at doSomething
```

When used at the beginning of a function only the code inside the function is in strict mode.

```
function doSomething() {
  "use strict";
  x = 1;
}
```

```
function doSomethingElse() {
  y = 1;
}

doSomethingElse();
console.log(y);
//1

doSomething();
//Uncaught ReferenceError: x is not defined
```

The strict mode also eliminates some JavaScript silent errors. Changing a frozen object throws an error instead of silently ignoring the change.

```
"use strict";

const obj = Object.freeze({});
obj.value = 1;
//Cannot add property value, object is not extensible
```

All the code from a class or a module is automatically in the strict mode. The majority of projects these days have the module system enabled and as such, they work in strict mode.

Key Notes

- A variable can have block, function, module, or global scope.
- Variables and functions defined in a module need to be exported in order to be accessible from other modules.
- Variables and parameters defined in a function are visible only inside that function.
- Variables defined in a block with `let` and `const` are visible only inside that block.
- Nested scopes create a scope chain. Every scope has a link to the parent scope.
- Lexical scope defines how variables and parameters are resolved in nested scopes. The inner scopes have access to variables and parameters from the parent scopes even if the parent scopes have existed.

Chapter 24: JSON

JSON is a text format for storing and transporting data. Its name comes from JavaScript Object Notation.

It is usually used to transfer data from the server to the web application.

The JSON format is similar to the object literal syntax and therefore is easier to convert the JSON strings into native JavaScript objects.

The JSON strings are made of name-value pairs. In each pair, the name always stays inside double-quotes, then there is a colon, followed by the value. Here is a simple JSON having two properties, one storing a string the other holding a number.

```
{
  "name": "The Cherry Orchard",
  "premiered" : 1904
}
```

The primitive types that can be represented in JSON are strings, numbers, booleans, and `null`. `undefined` is not a valid JSON value.

Strings should always use double quotes. We cannot define string values using single quotes or the backtick character.

The JSON objects are defined inside curly braces and can have several name-value pairs. Here is JSON that has a property storing an object.

```
{
  "author" : {
    "firstName" : "Anton",
    "lastName": "Cehov"
  }
}
```

JSON arrays are defined inside square brackets. An array can contain several values. A value can be a primitive or an object.

Next is simply JSON storing an array of numbers.

```
[1, 2, 3, 4, 5]
```

Below is an array of objects.

```
[
  { "name": "Three Sisters" },
  { "name": "The Cherry Orchard" },
  { "name": "Ivanov" }
]
```

Transforming into Objects

The JSON.parse utility parses a JSON string and returns the represented object.

```
const jsonText = '{"name": "The Cherry Orchard"}';

const play = JSON.parse(jsonText);
//{name: "The Cherry Orchard"}
```

If the JSON string is invalid JSON.parse throws an exception. Here is an example of parsing such a string.

```
const play = JSON.parse("");
//Unexpected end of JSON input at JSON.parse
```

Transforming into JSON Strings

The JSON.stringify function converts an object or a value to a JSON string.

```
const play = {
  name : 'Ivanov',
  author : 'Chekhov'
}

const json = JSON.stringify(play);
//'{"name":"Ivanov","author":"Chekhov"}'
```

We get an error when trying to transform into a JSON string an object with circular dependencies. Consider the following play object. It keeps a reference to the author object in the `author` property. The author object itself has a reference to the play object stored in the `lastPlay` property.

```
const author = {
  name: "Anton Chekhov"
}

const play = {
  name : "The Cherry Orchard",
  author
}

author.lastPlay = play;

console.log(JSON.stringify(play));
//Converting circular structure to JSON
//starting at object ... property 'author'
//property 'lastPlay' closes the circle
```

JSON strings do not contain functions. Functions are ignored when converting to JSON strings.

```
const play = {
  name : "Platonov",
  author: "Chekhov",
  getFormattedTitle(){
    return `${this.name} by ${this.author}`;
  }
}

console.log(JSON.stringify(play));
//'{"name":"Platonov","author":"Chekhov"}'
```

Symbol key properties are ignored when serializing an object using the `JSON.stringify` utility.

```
const play = {
  [Symbol('name')] : "Platonov",
  author: "Chekhov",
}
```

```
console.log(JSON.stringify(play));
//'{"author":"Chekhov"}'
```

Deep-Cloning

The JSON utilities can be used for deep-cloning.

There are simple methods for cloning an object like the spread syntax or the Object.assign utility but both of them do shallow cloning.

Shallow cloning means creating a new object that has the same fields and values as the original object. However, if any of the fields are objects themselves, just the references are copied not the actual objects.

```
const play = {
  name : 'Ivanov',
  author : {
   name: 'Chekhov'
  }
}
```

```
const clone = { ...play }
console.log(clone)
//{
//author: {name: "Chekhov"},
//name: "Ivanov"
//}
```

```
play.author.name = "Anton Chekhov";
```

```
console.log(clone)
//{
//author: {name: "Anton Chekhov"},
//name: "Ivanov"
//}
```

As you can see changing the name in the original author object affects also the clone.

Deep cloning means creating a new object with all the fields and values from the original object. If any of these fields is an object then new copies of those objects are created. The deep clone and the original object do not share any objects between them.

By first converting an object to a JSON string and then back to an object we can do deep cloning. Below is an example.

```
const play = {
  name : 'Ivanov',
  author : {
    name: 'Chekhov'
  }
}

const clone = JSON.parse(JSON.stringify(play));

play.author.name = "Anton Chekhov";

console.log(clone)
//{
//author: {name: "Chekhov"},
//name: "Ivanov"
//}
```

This time changing the name in the original author object does not affect the clone.

Key Notes

- JSON is a text format.
- JSON strings can be parsed into objects using the `JSON.parse` utility.
- Objects can be transformed into JSON strings with the `JSON.stringify` helper.
- By first converting an object into a string and then back to a new object we can build a deep clone.

Chapter 25: Asynchronous Model

JavaScript is a single-threaded programming language meaning that a single instruction can be executed at a specific time. The browser can use several threads but the program runs in a single thread.

This means we don't have to worry about mutex, semaphores, shared memory resource locking, and other things related to thread programming. It also means that we cannot do long operations without blocking the single thread.

Here is an operation blocking the thread for a few seconds.

```
function doOperation() {
  for (i = 0; i < 900719925; i++) {}
}

console.log("start")
doOperation();
console.log("end");
```

Below is a long operation making the web page unresponsive. The user is not able to interact with the webpage until the operation is completed.

```
function doLongOperation() {
  for (i = 0; i < Number.MAX_SAFE_INTEGER; i++) {}
}

doLongOperation();
```

Synchronous Functions

A synchronous function is one that returns only after the work is completed. This kind of function is easier to work with because when it returns we have access to the result.

Here is an example.

```
function max(a, b) {
  return a > b ? a : b;
}

const result = max(1, 2);
console.log(result);
//2
```

Next, let's consider what it means to wait for the user before returning the result.

confirm

The `confirm(message)` utility displays a box asking the user to accept or cancel something. It takes a message that is shown in the confirmation dialog.

The user has to click either OK or Cancel in order to continue. When the user clicks OK the function returns `true`, otherwise, it returns `false`.

```
const result = confirm("Are you sure?");
console.log(result);
```

The `confirm` function is a synchronous function. Everything is blocked until the user inputs the answer.

The same thing happens when using the `alert` and `prompt` utilities. Everything is blocked.

The `alert(message)` utility shows an alert dialog with the given message and an OK button.

The `prompt(message)` utility displays a dialog with an optional message asking the user to write a text. It returns the text entered by the user, or `null`.

As you notice the user is not able to do anything else but giving an answer. Even if the synchronous code logic is easier to understand for the developer it is not a great experience for the user.

Asynchronous Functions

Asynchronous function on the other hand return immediately and we can get the result somewhere in the future. Reading the result "somewhere in the future" makes it more difficult to work with.

Timers

JavaScript has two timer functions `setTimeout` and `setInterval`.

`setTimeout` allows invoking a function after a specific interval. The function is only executed once.

Below is an example of calling a function after 3000 milliseconds. 1000 milliseconds are 1 second.

```
setTimeout(() => {
  console.log('run')
}, 3000);
//'run' after 3s
```

We can prevent the scheduled callback from being executed using the `clearTimeout` function.

The `clearTimeout` utility removes the timer event created with the `setTimeout` function. The timer id returned by `setTimeout` is used as an argument for the `clearTimeout` utility.

The following function does not run in 3 seconds because the timer event is canceled.

```
const timerid = setTimeout(() => {
    console.log('run')
}, 3000);

clearTimeout(timerid);
```

`setInterval` enables us to invoke a function at the giving interval.

The next function executes every 3 seconds. The first call is not done immediately but after 3 seconds.

```
setInterval(() => {
  console.log('run')
```

```
}, 3000);
```

The `setInterval` timer invokes the function until `clearInterval` is called, or when the window is closed. The following function is not called because the `setInterval` timer event is canceled.

```
const timerid = setInterval(() => {
  console.log('run')
}, 3000);

clearInterval(timerid);
```

Both utilities take the same parameters. The first one is the callback function to be invoked, the second parameter is the time interval in milliseconds. The second parameter is optional and if omitted defaults to 0.

When scheduled to execute in 0 seconds the function is not executed immediately but as soon as possible, which is around 10 milliseconds when the thread is not busy.

Consider the following code. The numbers appear in reverse order. Even if `setTimeout` seems to execute immediately, that is not the case.

```
setTimeout(()=>{
  console.log(1);
}, 0);

console.log(2);

//2
//1
```

console.log

`console.log` is a built-in function that can be used to output values. In the browser, the output is displayed in the console tab, available from the Developer Tools.

The `console.log` utility function is not standardized so it may happen that the browser treats `console.log` as an asynchronous function. For example, the `console.log` utility may not log immediately the given input. Consider the next example.

```
const obj = {
```

```
  value : 1
};
```

```
console.log(obj);
obj.value = 100;
```

Even if the object is modified after the `console.log` call we may see the following result in the console.

```
{ value : 100 }
```

When encountering this issue, a solution may be to log a copy of the object or its JSON string representation.

```
console.log({...obj});
console.log(JSON.stringify(obj));
```

Callbacks

Consider the following synchronous function. Once it is called the result is returned and can be stored in a variable.

```
function getName(idx){
  return `Item ${idx}`;
}
```

```
const name = getName(1);
//'Item1'
```

The asynchronous equivalent function can be something like this.

```
function getName(idx){
  setTimeout(()=>{
    return `Item ${idx}`;
  }, 1000)
}
```

```
const name = getName(1);
//undefined
```

The problem this time is that we get **undefined** when trying to retrieve the result in a similar way as we did when using a synchronous function.

A common solution to this challenge is to pass a function to be called with the computed result. The function passed as an argument is called a callback.

Consider the next function that accepts a callback function as an argument. It computes the result and invokes the callback with it.

```
function getName(idx, callback){
  setTimeout(() => {
    callback(`Item ${idx}`);
  }, 1000)
}
```

We can now define a function that takes a value as a parameter and logs it to the console.

```
function logResult(name){
  console.log(name);
}
```

Then we can use the `logResult` function as a callback. After 1 second the `logResult` function is called with the computed name `'Item 1'`.

```
getName(1, logResult);
//'Item 1' after 1s
```

We can also create the callback one on the fly using the arrow syntax.

```
getName(1, name => {
  console.log(name);
});
```

Event Loop

Another important concept of the asynchronous model is the event loop.

The event loop is responsible for executing the code, registering and processing events.

The event loop uses a queue. When events occur messages are added to the event queue. Each message has an associated callback function that is invoked when processing it.

The first message is the first one to be processed and removed from the queue. The callback function runs to completion before another message is processed. All the messages in the event queue are processed until the queue is empty. Then are other messages are added and the processing starts again.

Calling setTimeout(callback, 1000) does not execute the callback in one second, but it just adds the callback to the event queue after one second. If there is nothing to be executed at that moment it will be called immediately, otherwise, its execution is delayed until all the other messages are processed.

Consider the following setTimeout calls.

```
function doOperation() {
  console.time()
  for (i = 0; i < 900719925; i++) {}
  console.timeEnd()
}

setTimeout(doOperation, 0);
setTimeout(doOperation, 0);
setTimeout(doOperation, 0);
console.log("all started");

//all started
//1404.424072265625 ms
//1379.698974609375 ms
//1515.298828125 ms
```

The three calls of the doOperation are not executed in parallel but one after the other. Three entries are added to the event queue.

Key Notes

- A synchronous function returns only after its work is completed. It blocks the thread until the work is done.
- An asynchronous function starts a task that will finish somewhere in the future and returns immediately. It does not block the thread.
- setTimeout registers a function to be called once after a specified time interval.
- setInterval registers a function to be called repeatedly at a given time interval.
- A callback is a function passed as an argument to another function.

Chapter 26: Automatic Type Conversion

The automatic type conversion also called "type coercion" is one of the dangerous parts of JavaScript.

The mathematical operators, do an automatic type conversion to the number type when applied to a non-numeric type.

```
'2' - 1
//1
```

```
'1' * 2
//2
```

```
true - 1
//0
```

```
'two' - 1
//NaN
```

To make things worse JavaScript has the same operator for both addition and concatenation. What does it mean to "add" two arrays?

```
[] + []
//''
```

In fact the + operator in the previous example does not "add" but it "concatenates" strings. So the correct question is what does it mean to concatenate the strings computed from two arrays.

When we convert an empty array to a string the result is an empty string.

```
String([])
```

```
//''
```

So concatenating the strings got from two such arrays results in `'' + ''` which is a new empty string.

Below is another example of what happens when JavaScript tries to do the automatic type conversion.

```
true + 1
//2
```

```
{} + []
//0
```

```
1 + '2'
//'12'
```

When comparing values of different types the double equal operator (`==`) uses a confusing and complicated conversion algorithm. Here are some "interesting" expressions evaluated as `true`.

```
null == undefined
1 == '1'
[] == ![]
```

The main idea is that is better to stay away from the unpredictable results of the coercion system.

Below are a few tips on how to avoid coercion in JavaScript.

Converting Operands to Numbers

Arithmetic is done with numbers. We need to make sure all operands are numbers before starting the computation. Take for example the trivial sum function.

```
function sum(x, y){
   return x + y;
}
```

```
sum('1', 2);
//'12'
```

The `Number` built-in function can convert any value into a number. The following `sum` function converts the operands to numbers before doing the computation.

```
function sum(_x, _y){
  const x = Number(_x);
  const y = Number(_y);
  return x + y;
}

sum('1', 2);
//3
```

Using Template Strings for Concatenation

As already said, the fact that + is both the addition and concatenation operator creates confusion especially when it comes together with coercion.

What does it mean 1 + '2' ?

- Should both operands be converted to numbers and use + as the addition operator, meaning 1 + 2 === 3?
- Should both operands be converted to strings and use + as the concatenation operator, meaning '1' + '2' === '12'?
- Or should the language throw an error saying that numbers cannot be added or concatenated to strings?

JavaScripts decides to do concatenation.

In Elixir string concatenation is done with <> operator.

```
iex> "1" <> "2"
# "12"
```

An exception is thrown when trying to concatenate a number to a string.

```
iex(1)> 1 <> "2"
# expected binary argument in <> operator but got: 1
```

Also an exception is thrown when trying to add a string to a number.

```
iex> 1 + "2"
# bad argument in arithmetic expression: 1 + "2"
```

In conclusion, it is better to use + for addition in JavaScript and use another syntax for concatenation. The intention of the code will be clearer this way.

Here is how we can replace the concatenation done with the + operator with the template string syntax.

```
1 + "2"  ===  `${1}${"2"}`
```

Instead of writing a + b when our intention is to do concatenation we should write `${a}${b}`.

When we read a + b we expect the program to do addition. When we get across `${a}${b}` it means that this time we want to do concatenation.

Using the Triple Equal Operator for Equality

According to the double equal operator [] is not equal to itself but is equal to ![] and even to `false`.

```
[] == ![]    //true
[] == false //true
```

As you have already seen the double equal operator considers a number to be equal to its string representation.

```
1 == "1"    //true
```

The double equal operator is not even transitive.

```
'0' == 0    //true
  0 == ''    //true
'0' == ''    //false
```

The triple equal operator should be used instead of the double equal operator. It does no automatic type conversion and is transitive.

```
1 === '1'        //false
[] === []        //false
[] === ![]       //false
[] === false     //false
```

Some programmers think that we have type coercion because JavsScript has dynamic typing. These other two different features of the language. We can very well have a language with dynamic typing without this automatic type conversion.

The automatic type conversion depends on how operators are handled. For example, 1 + '2' results in '12' because the language decides to make the automatic conversion when evaluating the plus (+) operator. It can very well decide to throw an exception. Elixir is a dynamically typed language and as you have seen it throws an exception when trying to add a string to a number.

Key Notes

- All arithmetic operators, except the plus operator that is more difficult, do an automatic type conversion to a number.
- The plus operator has a confusing type conversion algorithm to numbers or strings.
- The double equal operator has a complex automatic type coercion algorithm resulting in unexpected results.
- Convert operands to numbers in an arithmetic operation.
- Use template strings for concatenation.
- Use the triple equal operator for equality.

Chapter 27: Core Features

In this last chapter, we will look at the core and most important features of JavaScript.

Functions as Independent Units

Functions are units of behavior, but the important part here is that they are independent. In other languages like Java or C#, functions must be declared inside a class. This is not the case in JavaScript.

Functions can be declared in the global scope or defined inside a module as independent units that can be reused.

Objects as Dynamic Collections of Properties

Objects are just collections of properties. In other languages, they are called maps, hash maps, or dictionaries.

They are dynamic in the sense that, once created, properties can be added, edited, or deleted.

Below is a simple object defined using the object's literal syntax. It has two properties.

```
const series = {
  title: 'Star Trek',
  genre: 'SF'
}
```

Objects Inheriting From Other Objects

In class-based languages like Java or C# classes inherit from other classes. Again, that is not the case in JavaScript.

Objects inherit from other objects called prototypes.

In this language, objects are collections of properties. When creating an object, it has a "hidden" property called __proto__ that keeps a reference to another object. The referenced object is called a prototype.

Most objects inherit from the Object.prototype object.

```
const obj = {};
obj.__proto__ === Object.prototype;
//true
```

On our object, we can access, for example, the toString method even if we haven't defined such a method. This method is inherited from the Object.prototype. When trying to access the method, the engine first tries to find it on the current object, then it looks at the properties of its prototype.

Functions as Values

Functions are values in JavaScript. Like other values, they can be assigned to variables.

```
const sum = function(x,y){ return x + y }
```

This is not something that can be done in any language.

Like other values, functions can be passed to different functions or returned from functions. Below is an example of a function returning another function.

```
function startsWith(text){
  return function(name){
    return name.startsWith(text);
  }
}
```

```
const games = ['Fornite', 'Overwatch', 'Valorant'];
const newGames = games.filter(startsWith('Fo'));
console.log(newGames);
//["Fornite"]
```

In the same example, we can see how the returned function from the startsWith function is sent as an argument to the filter array method.

Closures

Functions can be defined inside other functions. The inner function can reference variables and parameters from the other functions.

The inner function can access variables and parameters from the outer function even after the outer function has been executed. Below is an example of this.

```
function createCounter(){
  let x = 0;
  return function(){
    x = x + 1;
    return x;
  }
}

const count = createCounter();
count(); //1
count(); //2
count(); //3
```

The `count` function has access to the `x` variable from the `createCounter` parent function even after it has been executed. `count` is a closure.

Almost Everything is an Object

JavaScript gives the illusion that primitives are objects by making them look as such. The fact is that primitives are not objects. Primitives are not collections of properties.

However, we can call methods on primitives. For example, we can invoke the `toUpperCase` method on a string:

```
const upperText = 'Minecraft'.toUpperCase();
//'MINECRAFT'
```

A simple text like `'Minecraft'` is a primitive and has no methods. JavaScript converts it into an object using the built-in `String` constructor and then runs the `toUpperCase` method on the newly created object.

By converting primitives to wrapper objects behind the scenes, JavaScript allows us to call methods on them and thus giving the illusion that they are objects.

Functions are also objects. They have properties like `name`, `call`, or `apply`.

Dynamic Typing

Variables, parameters, properties inherit the type of their values.

Here is a data object containing the `value` property storing a number.

```
const dto = { value: 1 };
```

Below is a similar object storing a string in the `value` property.

```
const dto = { value: 'text'}
```

The type of a variable, parameter, or property may change based on the type of value they store.

Constants don't change their type. We can avoid changing the type of a property by freezing the object at creation.

Below is an example of a function that can be called with any kind of value. If the value has the `name` property then it returns that property otherwise it gives `undefined`.

```
function getName(value){
  return value?.name;
}

getName({name: 'Darth Vader'});
//'Darth Vader'

getName(null);   //undefined
getName(0);      //undefined
getName('');     //undefined
```

The function works with any kind of object that has the `name` property. It does not matter if it is a game or movie object.

```
const gamesArr = [
  { name: 'Tzolkin' },
  { name: 'Catan' }
];


gamesArr.map(getName);
```

```
//["Tzolkin", "Catan"]

const moviesArr = [
 { name: 'Revenge of the Sith', genre: 'fantasy' },
 { name: 'A New Hope', genre: 'fantasy' }
];

moviesArr.map(getName);
//["Revenge of the Sith", "A New Hope"]
```

Single-Threaded Language

JavaScript is single-threaded. It means that only one statement is executed at a specific time.

Two functions cannot execute at the same time in the main thread.

This makes things easier to understand and we just have to pay attention to make functions run fast. A function that takes a long time to execute will make the page unresponsive.

Key Notes

- Functions are independent units of behavior.
- Objects are dynamic collections of properties.
- Objects inherit from other objects.
- Functions are values.
- Functions can be closures.
- Almost everything is an object, even primitives look like objects.
- Variable, properties, parameters can store values of any type.
- JavaScript is a single-threaded language.

What's next?

For a more in-depth look at JavaScript and main functional principles, you may read 'Discover Functional JavaScript'. Here, you will find more on pure functions, immutability, currying, decorators but also ideas on how to make code easier to read. JavaScript brings functional programming to the mainstream and offers a new way of doing object-oriented programming without classes and prototypes.

In the 'Functional Programming in JavaScript' book you will find how to use JavaScript as a functional programming language by disabling the 'this' keyword and enforcing immutable objects with a linter. You will learn how to use statements like 'if' and 'switch' in a functional way, or how to create and use functors and monads. It turns out that JavaScript has everything it needs to be used as a functional language. We just have to remove features from the language.

If you want to learn how to build modern React applications using functional components and functional programming principles, you can consider reading 'Functional React, 2nd Edition'.

Continue your learning path with 'Functional Architecture with React and Redux' book, and put in practice what you learned by building several applications with an incremental level of complexity.

The functional architecture implies getting the initial state, showing it to the user using the view functions, listening for actions, updating the state based on those actions, and rendering the updated state back to the user again.

The 'Microblog React Project' book takes a project-based learning approach by engaging you in building a practical application. The reader will learn things on the way by developing different parts of this project. The Microblog application will be built using React with Hooks and libraries like Redux, Redux Thunk, Redux Toolkit, Material UI, or Axios.

The 'UI State Management' book gives you an overview of how state is managed by building a note-taking application with four different libraries. We start from an object-oriented approach using Svelte, centralize state with Vuex, then move to a functional approach with React and Redux, and in the end arrive at a solution using only pure functions with Elm.

Vue.js
Composition API

Cristian Salcescu

The Composition API provides a new way of managing reactivity. It is made of a set of Reactive API functions plus the facility to register lifecycle hooks. Understand better the reactivity system by building one from scratch and then implement a master-details functionality. Check how to manage state using the Composition API and then use it to implement a central store similar to Vuex.

Principles of Design Patterns

An introduction to
Object-Oriented
Programming with C#

Cristian Salcescu

The Principles of Design Patterns help you to write code that is flexible, reusable and easier to maintain. These principles are:

- Program to an interface, not an implementation

- Favor object composition over class inheritance

- Encapsulate the concept that varies

Interfaces enable polymorphic behavior. Factories hide the complexities of creating objects.

Enjoy the learning journey!

About the author

Cristian Salcescu is the author of Discover Functional JavaScript.
He is a technical lead passionate about front-end development and
enthusiastic about sharing ideas. He took different roles and participated
in all parts of software creation.
Cristian Salcescu is a JavaScript trainer and a writer on Medium.